Bosnia and Herzegovina

Bosnia and Herzegovina

BY JoAnn Milivojevic

Enchantment of the World
Second Series

Children's Press®

A Division of Scholastic Inc.

NEW YORK   TORONTO   LONDON   AUCKLAND   SYDNEY
MEXICO CITY   NEW DELHI   HONG KONG
DANBURY, CONNECTICUT

Frontispiece: Vendors in a public square in Sarajevo

Consultant: Warren Lerner, Center for Slavic, Eurasian, and East European Studies, Duke University, Durham, NC

Please note: All statistics are as up-to-date as possible at the time of publication.

Book production by Herman Adler Design

Library of Congress Cataloging-in-Publication Data

Milivojevic, JoAnn.
  Bosnia and Herzegovina / by JoAnn Milivojevic
      p. cm. — (Enchantment of the World. Second series)
  Includes bibliographical references and index.
    ISBN 0-516-24247-4
  Bosnia and Herzegovina—Juvenile literature. [1. Bosnia and Herzegovina.] I. Title. II. Series.
  DR1660 .M552004
  949.742—dc21   2002015581

CHILDREN'S PRESS and associated logos are trademarks and or registered trademarks of Scholastic Library Publishing. SCHOLASTIC and associated logos are trademarks and or registered trademarks of Scholastic Inc.
1 2 3 4 5 6 7 8 9 10 R 13 12 11 10 09 08 07 06 05 04

Bosnia and Herzegovina

Contents

Cover photo:
Mostar Bridge

Bosnia's coast

Slavic plaque

Wrapped

Bosnia has a sense of "wrapped" about it. Glorious mountains wrap around lush valleys. Majestic rivers wind around the land, providing water for people, crops, and creatures. People are quick to embrace one another, kissing cheeks when they meet. Children walk down the street with their arms slung around each other; they touch easily, comfortably. Bosnia's history seems to blanket everything and everyone; at times it brings comfort and pride, at times it brings heaviness and difficulty. Bosnia's neighboring countries have both embraced it like friends and choked it like enemies. All this and more makes Bosnia a culturally rich and fascinating land.

It's a land where film directors produce award-winning films on incredibly small budgets, where radio stations play quiet traditional folk songs and screaming heavy metal rock. Where children play games such as marbles, making up their own rules as children everywhere do. It's also a place where children have witnessed the horrors of war in their very own streets.

Bosnia has also been known for its religious tolerance. It was and is a place where many ethnic groups have celebrated their differences and embraced their similarities. Muslims, Christians,

Opposite: **Trees wrap around the town of Jablanica.**

Muslim worshippers leave their shoes outside a mosque in Bjelasnica.

Jews, Serbs, Croats, and Gypsies all live here—and they have far more in common than not.

Bosnia and Herzegovina make up a new country that is also very old. People have lived in this region since before the birth of Christ. Bosnia as a state emerged around the tenth century. It is located in southeast Europe and is part of a collection of countries called the Balkans. The Balkan countries share a historic tie to a number of empires. Centuries ago, the Ottoman/Turkish Empire ruled much of this region for a very long time. It was during the time of the Ottoman Empire that Bosnia was linked with its neighbor, Herzegovina, remaining so to this day. Through the years, several empires have passed across Bosnia's borders, and in the process they have added their own distinctive mark on its culture.

This stone slab, carved by the Romans, was found in Bosnia and depicts a winged man on horse.

People pass a war-damaged building, a reminder of the 1992–1995 war.

Bosnia was most recently a part of another country, Yugoslavia. It declared independence in 1991, but didn't officially achieve that status until 1995. The birth of any country does not happen easily and rarely happens without a fight. In the case of Bosnia, the war lasted three years, from 1992–1995. It involved neighboring republics, the European

Geopolitical map of
Bosnia and Herzegovina

community, the United States, and members of the United Nations. Today, more than ten years after the first bomb fell, Bosnia is still scuffed and torn from its years of war, but it is rebuilding and renewing.

Historically, Bosnia and Herzegovina were two separate regions. Bosnia, the larger of the two is in the north and smaller Herzegovina is in the southwest around Mostar. These two regions were joined together for the first time in the fourteenth century and have remained linked ever since. Today, the country is known as Bosnia and Herzegovina (BiH) or simply Bosnia for short.

After the 1992–1995 war, the borderlines inside Bosnia changed. The country was divided into two parts to reflect the majority of people who lived in those parts. One part is called the Republic of Srpska (RS), home to mostly Serbians. The other half is the Federation of Bosnia and Herzegovina (FBiH) where mostly Muslims and Croatians live.

The structure of Bosnia is similar to states within the United States. The Federation of Bosnia and Herzegovina and the Republic of Srpska are like two states within the country of Bosnia. Just as states have capitals and local governments, so do these entities. Unlike U.S. states, the Federation of Bosnia and Herzegovina and the Republic of Srpska have a lot more control over their regions than do states in the United States.

Land of Forests and Mountains

IN TOTAL LANDMASS, THE COUNTRY OF BOSNIA AND Herzegovina covers 19,741 square miles (51,129 square kilometers). The Federation of Bosnia and Herzegovina is the larger of the two territories, covering just over one half of the country.

The mountains that dominate this country are the Dinaric Alps. Though hilly throughout, the land changes dramatically between north and south. The north has lush forests, waterfalls, and valleys, while the southern region of Herzegovina is more arid (meaning dry). Some plants and animals live in both regions, while others live only in one of them.

Opposite: **The fertile
Neretva Valley**

This triangular country weaves around Croatia and the former Yugoslavia like a jagged slice of pie. Serbia and Montenegro hug the east and southeast. Croatia borders the north and wraps around Bosnia to the west and southwest. Look closely at the western edge and you'll see that a small strip of Bosnian land pokes into the Adriatic Sea. This stretch of coastline (about 12 miles or 20 kilometers in length) is Bosnia's only gateway to the sea. Waterways to the sea are important to countries because they provide access for shipping and receiving goods. The Adriatic Sea touches Italy and also flows into the Mediterranean, a huge body of water that connects European and African countries.

Bosnia has only 12 miles (20 km) of coastal land.

Mountains High

The height of mountains affect weather, plants, and animals. It also affects how and where people live. The higher you go, the lower the temperature and the fewer plants, animals, and people you'll find. In Bosnia and Herzegovina, you may see shepherds here and there in high mountain areas, but most people live at lower elevations. It's easier to live and farm the fertile lower valley lands than to live in the mountains. Living high atop a mountain may provide a magnificent view, but few roads and services such as telephones, electricity, and running water are available. Some shepherds still live in mountain huts, however, with few, if any, of these modern conveniences.

Skiers ride the chair lift up Mount Bjelasnica.

An exception to this higher-up-sparser-living rule is ski resorts. Bosnia is famous for its skiing and it has a number of popular mountain areas ideal for this sport. They include Bjelasnica, Jahorina, Cvrsnica, and Maglic. The world community found these beautiful mountain ranges perfect for the Olympic Games. Sarajevo hosted the Fourteenth Winter Olympic Games in 1984.

The Dinaric Alps

The Alps are Europe's most extensive mountain system. They run through many countries including parts of France, Italy, Switzerland, Germany, Austria, and Slovenia. The Dinaric Alps in Bosnia are a part of this huge European mountain system. They run north and south along the eastern coast of the Adriatic Sea and expand horizontally into Bosnia. On a north-south axis, the range extends about 400 miles (644 km) from Slovenia to Albania.

Sprinkled throughout the Bjelasnica mountain region are traditional villages, watermills, mountain huts, canyons, waterfalls, and crystal clear lakes. If you were to venture above the treeline (5,000 feet/1,500 meters), you'd be treated to a panoramic vista of rocky peaks. You might also see the wolves, wild boar, and bears that call these rugged mountainsides home.

Bosnia is rich in natural resources and spectacular scenery. The country is working hard to implement nature conservation laws to help protect the countryside and to attract the growing number of eco-tourists to its beautiful land. Eco-tourists are travelers who especially enjoy nature and outdoor activities such as hiking and bird watching.

Sutjeska National Park is Bosnia's oldest national park. It is home to the republic's highest peak, Mount Maglic, which rises 7,828 feet (2,386 m). Mount Maglic is located in the southeast section of Herzegovina. Sutjeska also holds cultural and historical value. This rough terrain helped local soldiers defeat Germans during World War II. Terrain often plays a part in such conflicts. Because people who live on the land know the land well, they can often more easily defeat intruders by strategically using the land to outwit their enemies. For example, local soldiers know best where to place traps, the easiest ways to cross rivers, and how to hide and pass through caves.

Remnants of War

Unfortunately, land mines and booby traps left behind from the 1992–1995 war plague the countryside. Bosnia and Herzegovina is littered with millions of these devices, which hurt wild animals and make it impossible to walk safely in certain areas. The country continues to work to remove these remnants of war. In some areas, mine warning signs disrupt what is otherwise a peaceful countryside.

Taking a Look at Bosnia's Cities

Banja Luka (population 218,436), a city in northern Bosnia, is the capital of the Republic of Srpska. The majority of the population is Serbian in ethnicity. The city sits along the Vrbas River. Banja Luka is a major transportation hub with a railroad terminal and airport. It is the main business center of the Republic of Srpska and has highly developed agriculture, industry, and services sectors. During the 1992–1995 war, most of the town's mosques were destroyed. The ruins of a Roman fort and Roman baths still stand. The word *banja* means "spa" in the Serbian language and Banja Luka has several natural mineral spas nearby. The city's climate is continental, with temperatures around 70°Fahrenheit (21°Celsius) in July and 32°F (0°C) in January.

Mostar (population 208,904) is the main city in Herzegovina and has a mostly Croat and Muslim population. Mostar comes from the word *Mostari* meaning those who guard the bridge. The centuries-old bridge (below) built in 1566 by Ottoman sultan Sulayman the Magnificent, arches over the Neretva River. It stood for centuries until 1993 when bombs destroyed it. The bridge has since been rebuilt. Compared to the northern areas, the seasons are milder in Mostar with temperatures averaging in the 40s (5°C) in January and 80s (27°C) in July. The city is surrounded by high barren mountains.

Bihac (above) (population 52,971), measuring about 281 square miles (730 sq km), is located in the northwest on the border with Croatia. The city sits along a large river, the Una. The river is used for transportation and recreation such as fishing and swimming. A Turkish fortress dating to the sixteenth century shows that this town has been populated for hundreds of years. During the 1992–1995 war, the city was the site of intense fighting between Serbs and Bosnian-Croat forces.

Products made in Bihac include textiles, concrete, and agricultural foodstuffs. A university in the city specializes in mechanical engineering and education degrees. The weather is continental; in July temperatures average about 70°F (21°C) and in January 32°F (0°C).

Mountains Moving

What formed the Dinaric Alps (and all mountains) is essentially the same thing that moves the earth's crust today: the shifting of the continental plates. When plates deep inside the earth collide, the energy of the collision forces them upward. The ground above moves and rises to form mountains and other phenomena such as earthquakes. Bosnia and Herzegovina are very susceptible to earthquakes because the land has a number of fault lines (fractures in the earth's crust).

An earthquake destroyed most of the buildings in Banja Luka in 1969. Much of the city was rebuilt, only to be damaged again by the hands of man during the 1992–1995 war.

Lakes, Rivers, and Healing Waters

Water flows throughout Bosnia in many shapes and qualities. Mountains capture moisture in the form of rain and snow. The water runs through the rocks and flows into rivers and lakes.

Lake Jablanica is an important water reserve, as well as a major tourist center.

Some water remains underground, creating huge subterranean lakes and streams. These underground rivers can snake for miles and miles and suddenly pop up to create a lake.

Some lakes in Herzegovina are seasonal. They develop in winter when the snow melts and underground rivers flood and force water up. In drier summer months, these lakes completely disappear.

The waters around Bosnia have many uses. People enjoy rivers and lakes for recreational purposes such as swimming, fishing, and boating, and also rely on rivers for transporting goods. Some waters are also beneficial to one's health. The waters that flow through mountain rocks absorb valuable minerals, making them good for drinking and bathing. Factories bottle mineral waters for drinking, and some areas have naturally occurring hot and cold springs, where health spas have arisen. The waters are believed to help relieve stress and heal certain health problems. Just outside the capital city of Sarajevo, for example, is Kiseljak, a popular cold spring health spa. The temperature of the water is a cool 53°F (12°C). People often fill bottles with this water for home use.

Six major rivers flow through Bosnia and Herzegovina: the Neretva, Sava, Drina, Bosna, Una, and Vrbas. The last four are tributaries of the great Sava River, which joins the mighty Danube River and flows east, emptying into the Black Sea.

Only one river flows south into the salty Adriatic Sea—the Neretva River. The mouth of this river is the republic's only outlet to the sea. The Neretva River is important for another reason. It has been designated by the United Nations Educational, Scientific, and Cultural Organization (UNESCO) as an international natural monument.

Europe's longest subterranean river, the Trebisnjica, flows through Bosnia and emerges in Dubrovnik, Croatia. The strength and speed of the Trebisnjica has been harnessed to produce electric power for Dubrovnik and other nearby towns. The river is so powerful the country built a 400-foot (122-m) tall concrete flood-gate close to the town of Trebinje in Herzegovina to dam the river.

Glacial lakes, which are products of melted ice caps, are numerous in Bosnia. Prokosko, a glacial lake, contains rare species of salamanders and trout. The lake has a deep blue hue, and its water overflows and creates creeks and small rivers.

The Neretva River is not only a tributary to the Sava River, but has been designated as an international monument.

Rocks Exposed

The Dinaric Alps are composed of limestone and dolomite. The limestone here is a byproduct of coral reefs. Some 200 million years ago, during the Mesozoic Era, this region was underwater. Coral thrived in the warm water. Corals are small creatures with skeletons made of calcium carbonate, the main component of limestone. The corals lived together in tight colonies called coral reefs, which are essentially limestone structures. Over millions of years, the land shifted and the waters receded, leaving behind these limestone-rich mountains.

Limestone is very porous and is slowly dissolved by water. These porous rocks can also store petroleum, natural gas, and water. Limestone rocks, melted down by eons of rain and carved out by underground rivers, become a barren, lumpy countryside that resembles the landscape of the moon. This landscape is called *karst*. Its geographical features include limestone ravines, sink holes, caves, and underground streams. Herzegovina is classic karst country. Little grows in this barren region except scrub brush and drought-resistant grasses.

Bosnians endure harsh cold winters.

Climate

The climate in BiH is a combination of continental (also called temperate) and Mediterranean. The characteristics of a continental climate are warm humid summers and cold winters with snow. Such a climate also has four distinct seasons: spring, summer, autumn, and winter. Because air cools as it rises, the seasons are much different higher up in the Dinaric Alps compared to the lower elevations. Mountain summers are shorter and cooler, and mountain winters are longer and colder. The coastal Adriatic area has seasons that are best described as Mediterranean. The sea keeps temperatures more moderate, meaning that winters tend to be

milder and more rainy than temperate climates. Summers are
typically sunny and dry.

Bosnia's Geographical Features

Lowest Elevation:
City of Neum, sea level
(0 m)

Highest Elevation:
Maglic, 7,828 feet
(2,386 m)

Highest Waterfall:
Skakavac, 320 feet
(98 m)

Largest City: Sarajevo,
415,631 people

Highest Temperature:
Mostar, 100°F (38°C)
in July

Lowest Temperature:
Maglic mountain peak,
-4°F (-20°C) in January

Largest Artificial Lake:
Jablanicko

**Longest Underground
River:** Trebisnjica

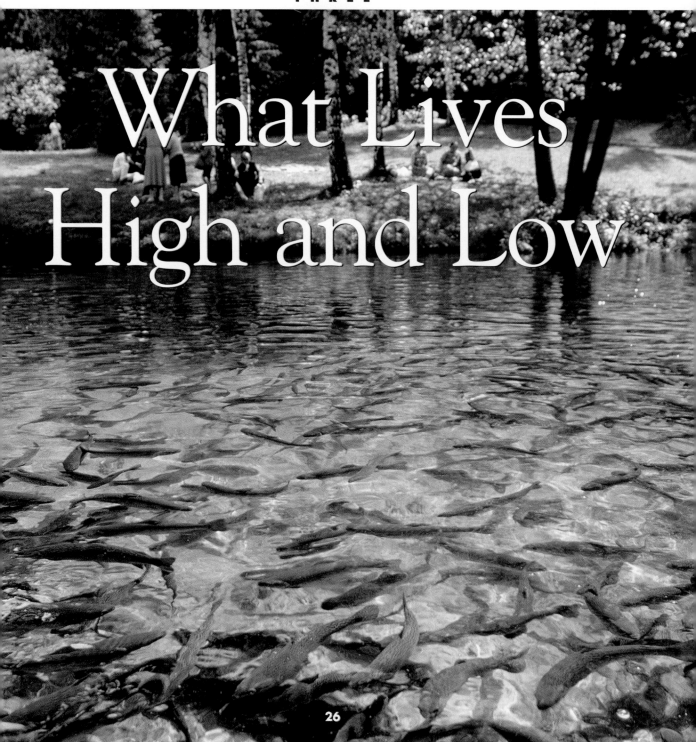

What Lives
High and Low

BOSNIA HAS MOUNTAINS, VALLEYS, BARREN ROCKY LAND-scapes, and a small strip of salty seacoast. With different landscapes, soils, elevations, and climates come a variety of plants and animals. About 3,500 species of flora grow in the region. Wild plants and animals as well as farm-based creatures and crops inhabit the country.

Elevation is just one factor that affects everyday life. For example, mountain tops generally have lower temperatures and higher precipitation than lower lands. The flora and fauna on mountains must be able to thrive in cold, wet environments. Some plants and animals can adapt to many types of

Opposite: **A school of fish in a Bosnian river**

Signs of Weather and Seasons

By watching plants and animals, people in Bosnia forecast weather and seasons. In the hills and valleys, the blooming of *visibaba* (snowdrop plant) (pictured), a small, pretty white flower, signals that spring is on its way. Farmers say that when chickens cluck and run around wildly, it's a sign of bad weather. If insects become more active and bees return to their hives, locals say rain will soon come.

terrain, and to the changing seasons, by dropping leaves, shedding fur, or molting feathers. Other life exists exclusively in certain zones because those areas have the appropriate temperatures and climate. For example, olive trees thrive in arid, warm weather. They grow in the drier southern region of Herzegovina but not in the northern regions of Bosnia.

Mountain Wild

Mountains, forests, hills, and valleys dominate most of Bosnia. Inside the forested regions are some unique plants and animals. Slithering through the woods is the dangerous horned viper, a poisonous snake with hollow fangs through which it shoots deadly venom. The venom is the snake's defense against predators and its method of killing prey before eating it.

Horned vipers make their home in Bosnia's forests.

Wild boars are common in Bosnia.

Four-legged wild animals include deer, fox, wild boar, lynx, squirrel, marten, and a particularly vicious brown bear that lives around the Nereteva River valley. A local legend says that this bear is so powerful that it can pull out a tree by its roots, just as we might pull a carrot out of the earth.

A lynx

The golden jackal is a small wild canine that hunts throughout Bosnia.

Pheasants are a common game bird found in the hills and valleys of Bosnia.

People keep dogs as pets in Bosnia and Herzegovina, but the area also has wild canines. A type of wild dog that lives in the mountains of Herzegovina is the golden jackal. It is about the size of a fox, standing 16 inches (40 centimeters) high and 28 inches (70 cm) in length. Its coarse coat is tawny red. Jackals eat many things including eggs, fish, frogs, and even small livestock such as chickens, if they can get them. Golden jackals mate for life with one partner and like dry open country, short grasslands, and steep terrain.

Eagles, hawks, pheasants, wild ducks, and storks are among the birds of Bosnia and Herzegovina. Farmers also raise chickens for eggs and as livestock. Bosnia and Herzegovina are also home to the red turtle which, like most turtles, hibernates during the winter.

A Balkan Landscape

The word *Balkan* means forested mountain, and it is a good description of the Bosnian landscape. Almost half of Bosnia is forested. As you cross the country from north to south, the forests change. In the north, thick strands of pine and hardwood trees cover the hills and mountains. In the dryer south, the forests have fewer trees. Also in the southern region are trees that prefer more arid climates, such as the olive tree.

Tree and plant types vary depending on how high up a mountain you go. Below 2,000 feet (609 m), you'll find linden, oak, maple, and beech trees. Above 4,000 feet (1,219 m) are mostly pine and fir trees. Some are very rare, such as the

Pine and fir trees grow at elevations above 4,000 feet (1,219 m) in the Bosnian mountains.

Hutovo Bloto National Park

Hutovo Bloto National Park, in the southern region of Herzegovina, encompasses 18,313 acres (7,411 hectares) and is a well-known stopping point for migratory birds. The lakes and rivers here are rich in eel, carp, and other freshwater fish. The birds feast on this bounty in the rivers.

Pancic Spruce that dates to the Tertiary Period, 26 to 66 million years ago. As you approach mountain peaks, vegetation thins significantly because the air is thinner, colder, and more windy. No trees grow in the high alpine zone, although you will see small plants. Many grow a type of fuzz that insulates them from the harsh weather.

Coastal Life

The 12 miles (19.3 km) of Adriatic coastline that belong to Bosnia have mild, rainy winters and hot, dry summers. Short shrubs, not trees, grow in this area because the shrubs have extensive roots and can better absorb moisture and nutrients from the soil than taller trees. The olive tree, common in the

The coastal area in Bosnia has dry warm summers.

coastal area and throughout Herzegovina, has light grey leaves that reflect the hot sun and cool the plant. Deer, rabbits, rodents, and many species of birds make their home along the coast. On hot days some animals, such as rabbits, burrow underground to escape the heat.

Cherries Sweet and Sour

People living in the hills around Herzegovina are quite proud of their cherries. They work hard to irrigate the cherry orchards, which are on terraces—hillside plots that cascade through the countryside. Some plots are named after their owners or describe the terrain; for example, a plot might be called, "rocky" or "Uncle Dragi." The cherries are usually one of four varieties, each ripening at a different time of year. The first to ripen are *aprilka* (*AH-preel-ka*). They are ready in April and have a sour taste. The sweetest cherries ripen later in the season. The *svabicas* (*SVAH-bee-kas*) are plump, almost black, and sticky sweet. To resist eating them, hired workers often sing while picking them—because if you are singing, you can't be eating.

Bosnia Through the Centuries

Hundreds of years ago in the time before Christ, people known as the Illyrians lived in present-day Bosnia and Herzegovina. Illyrians were people of Indo-European background. They were nomads who made their way to the Balkan region from central Asia around the seventh century B.C.E.

Their kingdom, called Illyria, existed for about a hundred years in southeastern Europe. Eventually, all of Illyria was absorbed into the Byzantine Empire (an offshoot of the Roman Empire). The Illyrians became part of the Byzantine Empire and adapted to its culture.

Opposite: **A UN soldier monitors activity in Sarajevo during the civil war.**

Pirates of the Adriatic

The Illyrians were notorious pirates who took over ships and raided villages along the Adriatic coast. The Illyrians established a kingdom in what is modern-day Albania. The Romans wanted the Illyrians to stop pirating Roman ships. When threats of war did not stop them from their high-seas stealing, the Romans invaded their capital twice, in 229 and 219 B.C.E. This finally brought the piracy to an end.

A collection of Slavic ornamental plaques dating from the sixth century.

In 6 C.E., another migrant group known as the South Slavs settled in the Balkan area. These people arrived from central Europe. Today's Serbs, Croats, Slovenes, and Bosnian Muslims are all of Slavic descent, meaning that they can trace their roots to these early tribes. These groups have different religious practices today but they all share a common ancestry.

The first reference to a "Bosnia" arose in the tenth century. During this time, the various Slavic tribes (primarily Serbs and Croats) became more defined and settled in particular regions. Croats claimed much of the northern and coastal lands, while the Serbs dominated the inlands. Though they shared Bosnia, they did not practice the same religion. After the Roman Empire split in two in 1054, the Croats became Christian Catholics and the Serbs Christian Orthodox. Catholicism influenced the Croat lands; the Eastern Byzantine Empire brought Orthodoxy to the Serbian regions.

Land Grabbers

Throughout its early life, Bosnia was surrounded by other empires. It was caught in a tug of war between several mighty forces whose rulers wanted the same land. Bosnia also wanted to expand its territory and stepped on the toes of the empires around it. Through the centuries, no less than four

The Great Schism of 1054

The Roman Empire at its peak had invaded so many lands that it needed two administrative centers to manage them all. The main center was based in Rome (above). The second center was in the East, in Constantinople (right) (today's Istanbul in Turkey). In 1054, the East split from the West and formed its own unit in what was called the Great Schism of 1054. The Byzantines became known as "Orthodox," while in Rome they were "Catholic." Though both were Christians, they had conflicting views on Christianity.

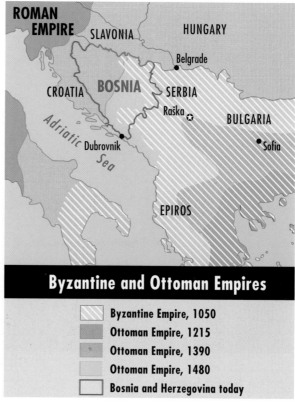

ROMAN EMPIRE
SLAVONIA
HUNGARY
Belgrade
CROATIA
BOSNIA
SERBIA
Raška
BULGARIA
Adriatic Sea
Dubrovnik
Sofia
EPIROS

Byzantine and Ottoman Empires

Byzantine Empire, 1050
Ottoman Empire, 1215
Ottoman Empire, 1390
Ottoman Empire, 1480
Bosnia and Herzegovina today

Matthias Corvinus, King of Hungary, ruled from 1443–1490. He built the most powerful kingdom in Central Europe.

empires sought to absorb this region: the Roman, Byzantine, Ottoman, and Austro-Hungarian.

Not long after Bosnia was recognized as Bosnia, the Hungarian Empire to the north became more powerful. They reached down to grab Slovenia, Croatia, and Bosnia. They ruled Bosnia from 1180–1463. But, given the mountainous terrain of Bosnia, it was difficult for the Hungarians to watch them very closely. At times Bosnia was able to slip out of Hungary's grasp and enjoy some years of independence.

Rulers in Bosnia were called *bans* (pronounced BAHns), a Hungarian term. Some bans remained loyal to Hungary, while some shifted their allegiance to Byzantine and Serbian

King of Bosnia

At the age of fifteen, a young boy named Tvrtko Kotromanic was crowned as Bosnia's first king. King Tvrtko governed Bosnia from 1353–1391. He threw off the shackles of Hungarian rule, conquered many lands, and made Bosnia the most powerful state in the region.

Trvtko first joined Bosnia to the principality of Hum (later known as Herzegovina). For a time, Tvrtko was called King of Bosnia and Raska (Serbian territory). After he died, the lands he united fell apart as others grabbed for power. Trvtko is remembered as Bosnia's finest king.

dynasties in nearby lands. Ban Kulin who ruled from 1180–1204, made Bosnia an independent land for the first time.

Religion Tangles with Politics

Ban Kulin rejected both the Catholic and Orthodox versions of Christianity, choosing instead a different type of Christianity called Bogomilism. This threatened the powers of the Roman and Byzantine Empires. Rome sought to stamp out Kulin and the Bogomils.

Under much pressure, Kulin rejected his Bogomil faith. But the faith had many followers and endured until the Ottoman Empire entered Bosnia and brought with it another religion, Islam. The Kulin years were good years economically. Kulin improved the local economy mainly by selling the rich minerals from Bosnia's mines.

Enter the Ottoman Empire

After King Tvrtko died, the subsequent rulers couldn't maintain Bosnia's independence for long. When the mighty force of the Ottoman army came to Bosnia's gates in 1463, Bosnia's rulers could do little to withstand it. The Ottomans (also

This map shows the western Ottoman Empire. Featured are settlements, distinct boundaries, roads, and topographical features.

called the Turks) invaded most of the Balkans, and ruled the region for almost 500 years.

The Ottoman Empire was vast—at one time it spanned three continents. As with other empires before it, the Ottoman reign would not last forever, but its influence extended beyond its final ruling years.

Even the Mighty will Fall

By the 1800s, the Ottoman Empire began to crumble. Its social system remained a closed society based on agriculture, but at the same time, the merchant and industrial revolution was sweeping across Europe. Only drastic change could save the Ottoman Empire. However, many of its officials didn't want change. They wanted to hold on to their power, positions, and land.

The sultan (or ruler) recognized that change had to occur—but the Bosnian elite resisted, threatening to wage war against him. Rebellions ate away at the empire. Meanwhile, outsiders such as the Russians and the Hungarians had their eyes on Bosnia as well. Nearby Serbia had ideas of creating a greater Serbia by claiming provinces within Bosnia with majority Serb populations. Croatia also wanted a piece of Bosnia for itself.

Bitter fighting took place in the streets of Sarajevo between Bosnian rebels and the Turkish government forces.

A Familiar Scene

The desire to divide Bosnia into ethnic-specific pieces was not just an ancient historic desire. It happened again in 1991, when the Croats and Serbs waged war to grab a part of Bosnia for themselves. Bosnian Muslims also joined the fight to claim pieces of it.

The Bosnian elites waged a war that lasted two years. In the end, the Ottoman army defeated the Bosnians, but not before they destroyed much of the land and property. Some changes did occur. Christians were given more rights and began to form a middle class. Still, many inequalities made people from all sides unhappy, including those who lost power and those who wanted more. The toll of civil wars, excessive debts owed to European powers, and continuing struggles with reform eventually wore down the Ottoman Empire, and it eventually lost its grip of Bosnia.

What the Ottoman Empire Left Behind

The Ottoman Empire made some positive contributions to life in Bosnia. In fact, some of its ideas and structures continue to influence life in Bosnia today. For example, the Ottomans established charitable foundations that provided food to needy people. Helping the poor is still part of culture and government programs today. The Ottomans also built roads between towns, many of which are still in use. The Empire's distinctive style of architecture, which features curved domes, can be seen all over the country. Mosques, houses of worship for Muslims, provide perfect examples of the elegant domed architecture (right).

Treaty of Berlin

In 1875, a peasant rebellion in Herzegovina spread into neighboring provinces and led to a war between Russia and Turkey that lasted from 1877 to 1878. At the war's end, the powers in charge met in Berlin, Germany, to negotiate a treaty. The greatly weakened Ottoman Empire lost a good deal of its territory. The Austro-Hungarian Empire was granted the right to send its army into the region on the condition that it protected Bosnia and Herzegovina from other intruders, such as Serbia and Croatia. It was a trick. The Austro-Hungarian Empire really wanted Bosnia for itself—and it took it in 1908.

Of World Wars and the Birth of Yugoslavia

Croatia and Serbia were tired of the Austro-Hungarian occupation of Bosnia. They realized that by uniting, they might both get what they wanted: independence from foreign rule.

Delegates greet each other at the Treaty of Berlin, which was held to stop Russian expansion into the Ottoman Empire.

The Austro-Hungarian flag is raised over a fort outside Sarajevo. The Turks were forced to abandon the city.

The seed was planted for what would become Yugoslavia, or "Land of South Slavs."

In 1908, Austria-Hungary was losing its power. So that other countries would not see them as weak, they occupied Bosnia and Herzegovina and claimed it as theirs—changing the rules set by the Treaty of Berlin. Austro-Hungarian administrators made laws that Bosnians were forced to obey. Hatred toward Austria hung in the air. Anti-Austrian groups formed, and one in particular would set off World War I.

Mlada Bosna (Young Bosnia) consisted of intellectuals who were against Austrian rule in Bosnia. A few disgruntled teenagers in the group took matters into their own hands. With the help of a radical group called the Black Hand, they plotted to assassinate the Austrian Archduke Franz Ferdinand and his military governor as they paraded through the streets of Sarajevo.

The Black Hand

The Black Hand was a secret society of Serbs who wanted to create a greater Serbia. They sought to unify all Serbs by any means they thought necessary, including violence. The group consisted mainly of military men, but it also included university professors, lawyers, and other professionals. In 1908, the Black Hand provided inside information regarding the Archduke's visit. They gave bombs and weapons to members of Mlada Bosna for the purpose of assassinating Ferdinand.

Political assassinations were common during the turn of the twentieth century. No less than forty world leaders, kings, and presidents (including U.S. president William McKinley) died at the hands of an assassin. When Ferdinand's entourage made a wrong turn in Sarajevo, Gavrilo Princip, a Serb member of Mlada Bosna, found himself almost face to face with the archduke. Princip aimed his gun and shot Ferdinand. He squeezed the trigger again, intending to shoot the military governor, but he killed Ferdinand's wife instead.

Europe was already unstable. Various nations were stockpiling weapons and political leaders were nervous. Although some countries made arms agreements, mistrust was high. The situation was like dry leaves waiting for a match— and the assassination of Ferdinand was that match. As a result of the killing, Austria declared war on Serbia. The conflict spread like wildfire. Eventually, thirty-two nations joined in the war, including the United States, Britain, France, Russia, and Germany.

Serb nationalist and member of the Black Hand, Gavrilo Princip, assassin of Archduke Franz Ferdinand

Nationalism and War

Among the leading causes of World War I were the rise in nationalism, economic trade disputes, and the stockpiling of weapons. The word *nationalism* refers to the building of a nation by uniting people of the same ideals and ethnic heritage. By the late 1800s, some people of like ethnicity battled and won their independence from occupying empires. New nation-states created in the late 1800s included Belgium, Italy, and Germany. However, many other independence-seekers had yet to achieve their goals. Chief among them were the Slavs in the Balkans and Bosnia. Many Slavs were eager to achieve independence. When Austria annexed Bosnia, the Serbs were angered. They wanted to create a larger Serbia and unite people of Slavic heritage, which included Croats, Slovenes, and Serbs.

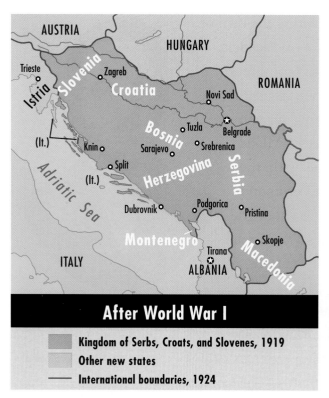

After World War I

Kingdom of Serbs, Croats, and Slovenes, 1919
Other new states
International boundaries, 1924

Above right: **Nazi Germans stand at attention in front of city hall in Sarajevo.**

World War I lasted four years (1914–1918). Its end also brought the end of the Austro-Hungarian Empire. The Kingdom of Serbs, Croats, and Slovenes emerged, and it included Bosnia and Herzegovina. In 1929, the kingdom was renamed Yugoslavia and included six republics: Serbia, Croatia, Bosnia and Herzegovina, Montenegro, Slovenia, and Macedonia.

World War II (1939–1945) brought more strife to Bosnia and Herzegovina. Germany invaded Yugoslavia and created its own Nazi state, under the title of the Independent State of Croatia. It was hardly independent, however. Instead, a fascist movement formed inside Croatia called the Ustasha. It was the terrorist force that had assassinated King Aleksandar of Yugoslavia in 1934. By the war's end, the Ustasha had rampaged through Yugoslavia. It is estimated that more than 300,000 Serbs, Jews, and Gypsies were murdered by the Utasha.

A Civil War Collides with the World War

As if it weren't enough to have outside forces waging war, Yugoslavia would endure a civil war at the same time. Two resistance groups within Yugoslavia challenged their German

Josip Broz Tito, dictator of Yugoslavia

occupiers. These two groups, the Chetnick (mostly Serbian) and the Partisans (a multi-ethnic communist group) fought not only the foreign invaders, but eventually each other as well. At the war's end, Josip Broz Tito, a Croat and leader of the Partisan party, took over as ruler of Yugoslavia.

Tito, a communist, ruled Yugoslavia by the philosophy "in the name of brotherhood and unity." In essence, the phrase was a call to set aside ethnic differences and unite for the good of all citizens. Tito proclaimed himself president for life. His dictatorship lasted thirty-five years.

The Socialist Federal Republic of Yugoslavia

Yugoslavia was one of the largest communist countries outside of the Soviet Union. Under communist rule, a government owns most of the country's land, factories, and resources. Tito ran the country with his own version of communism. This angered the Soviets, and they kicked him out of the communist community in 1948.

Life under Tito's regime was a blessing and a curse. Those who dared speak against Tito were imprisoned or killed. For the others, life was tolerable. Tito socialized healthcare so that all citizens has access to hospitals, medicines, and doctors. His welfare system helped ensure that the poor had food and

Refusing to Take Sides

During the cold war, which took place after World War II, the world had two main power blocs—the United States and the Soviet Union. Tito formed a nonaligned movement for countries that did not side with either bloc. This political movement earned him worldwide recognition.

shelter and allowed new mothers to take several months of paid leave after giving birth. Modern conveniences such as washers and refrigerators became commonplace in most homes. Women also gained some rights during the Tito years—they were encouraged to work, educate themselves at universities, and run for public office.

On the dark side, however, a secret police force helped prevent political opposition groups from forming. And though citizens were not forced to join the communist party, they certainly fared better if they did. The best jobs, homes, and privileges went to party members.

After Tito died in 1980, Yugoslavia dissolved into chaos. The economy had already begun to crumble and continued to deteriorate as politicians battled for power. The politicians quickly aligned themselves along nationalist lines (e.g., Croat, Serbian, Slovenian) and blamed one another for the country's economic troubles. When Slobodan Milosevic became president of Serbia in 1989, many republics, including Bosnia, were worried by his pro-Serb talks. They feared that Serbs would receive more rights and opportunities, and that their rights might be taken away. This was one of the reasons why Bosnia and other republics began to talk of independence.

The first to vote for independence was Slovenia in 1990. Croatia and Macedonia quickly followed. The few border battles were settled quickly. Within a year and half of settling the dispute with Croatia, however, about 300,000 people became refugees. Bosnia's fate was even worse.

Religion Takes a Back Seat

Under Tito, people were discouraged from practicing religion. Religious holidays such as Ramadan and Christmas were still celebrated, but people rarely attended regular religious services during the Tito years.

Ethnic Cleansing

During the war, Serbs and Croats wanted to rearrange the population. They believed that if they could move a majority of their people to one particular place, they could claim that place as part of their own republic. The term "ethnic cleansing" describes this process of forcing people out of their homes and removing any cultural essence of that group from the area, for example, destroying mosques and historical monuments of Muslims.

The High Price of Independence

Serbia and Croatia wanted to divide Bosnia and Herzegovina between themselves. When Bosnia declared independence and the European Community recognized it as such in March 1992, Serbs, Croats, and Bosnian Muslims went to war.

For three years the groups fought over Bosnia. War destroyed many of the buildings, homes, mosques, and churches of Bosnia. Croat and Serbian military groups within Bosnia sided with their nations, while the Muslims were divided between the two. At times, Croats and Serbs worked together to rid Bosnia of Muslims; at other times, Serbs and Muslims worked together to push Croats out. The Serbs had the power of the Yugoslav army behind them—at one time, the Serbs occupied nearly 70 percent of Bosnia.

The war was tragic for everyone in Bosnia. The country was heavily bombed. The horrors that were committed against

Forced From Their Homes

Refugees are people who are forced from their homelands by war or natural disasters. Many refugees from Bosnia have made new homes in other lands, including Canada and the United States of America. The United Nations Office of High Commissioner for Refugees helps settle displaced people. This international organization, as well as many others, helps people find new places to live.

civilians led to criminal indictments. The United Nations International Criminal Tribunal charged military leaders with crimes against humanity. More than 250,000 people had died and 1.8 million were displaced.

The Dayton Peace Agreement negotiated in 1995 in Dayton, Ohio, divided Bosnia into two entities: Croat-Muslim Bosnia and Herzegovina, and a Serb Republic called Republic of Srpska. To help ensure stability in the region, an international peace-keeping force remains in Bosnia as of 2003.

Bosnian president Alija Izetbegovic (left) shakes hands with Serbian president Slobodan Milosevic (right) as Croatian president Franjo Tudjman watches at the peace talks in Dayton, Ohio, 1995.

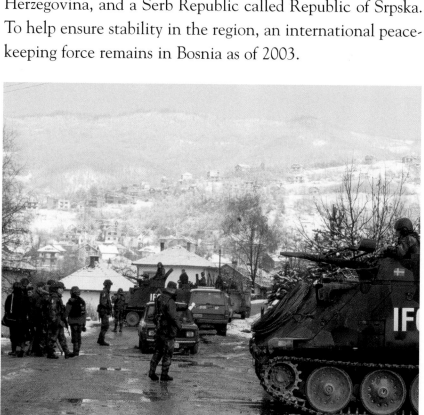

UN forces remain in Bosnia to ensure peace.

Forming a New Country

CONFÉRENCE DE PAIX SUR L
PARIS

I N 1995, AFTER FOUR YEARS OF WAR, THE POLITICAL LEADERS
representing the warring parties of the region negotiated
a truce, in Dayton, Ohio, in the United States. Slobodan
Milosevic was the leader of the Serbs, Alija Izetbegovic led
the Muslims, and Franjo Tudjman led the Croats. American
diplomat Richard Holbrooke helped bring these men together.
He and his staff kept the negotiations going. After weeks of dis-
cussions, the plan for the new country was formed and
approved. Today, BiH is considered a developing democracy.

Forming a country on paper is one thing, but making it
come true in real life is quite another. The post-war complica-
tions were many. Who would govern the country? How would
it be governed? How and who would rebuild war-damaged
roads, buildings, and factories? With emotions running
high, how could the country guard itself against reviving the
conflict? These were among the many questions the Dayton
Peace Accords attempted to answer.

Opposite: **World leaders at the signing of the Dayton Peace Agreement**

Alija Izetbegovic

A devout Muslim, lawyer, and political activist, Alija Izetbegovic was born in 1925 in Bosnanski Samac. In the 1980s he was imprisoned for plotting against the government of Yugoslavia. He rose to power in 1990 when his political party, the Muslim Party of Democratic Action, beat the communists in multiparty elections. He became president of Bosnia that year.

In 1996, after the civil war, he was re-elected as one of the three presidents in the new BiH. In 2000, however, he resigned from office for health reasons. Though out of the spotlight, he is still a political force in Bosnia.

The Dayton Peace Agreement

The Dayton Peace Agreement ended a conflict that killed more than 250,000 people and created 1 million refugees. The framework issued by the U.S. State Department on November 30, 1995 spelled out how each country needed to behave toward its fellow nations. In general, the plan required that Bosnia and Herzegovina, Croatia, and the Federal Republic of Yugoslavia had to respect one another's borders. When they disagreed, they had to settle peacefully.

The United Nations (UN) Security Council served as middleman among these countries. The UN helped keep peace and settle disagreements. Because so much anger existed among people's of these countries, the plan also required them to fully cooperate with the UN Security Council. Without full cooperation of all parties, lasting peace would not occur. Fortunately, the countries have cooperated, and as of 2003 the peace has not been interrupted.

Deal-Making in Dayton—Drafting Peace

Because everyone must compromise, no negotiated settlement makes all parties completely happy. It's a give-and-take process. Peace has taken hold in Bosnia, but its people and politicians continually work together to make it last. Cooperation and compromise are always necessary, as they are for all countries that seek a democratic government.

The Dayton Agreement laid a path for leaders to follow. It detailed government structure, land borders, election processes, the rights of refugees to return, how war criminals would be handled, reconstruction procedures, and how to organize a new military and police force.

The Government Today

Bosnia and Herzegovina has one central government and two semi-autonomous entities, each with its own local government. One entity is dominated by Serbs, Republic of Srpska. It consists of 49 percent of the land with sixty-three

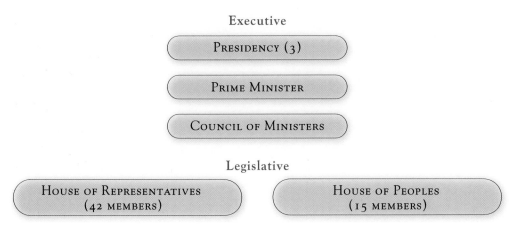

NATIONAL GOVERNMENT OF BOSNIA AND HERZEGOVINA

Executive

PRESIDENCY (3)

PRIME MINISTER

COUNCIL OF MINISTERS

Legislative

HOUSE OF REPRESENTATIVES (42 MEMBERS)

HOUSE OF PEOPLES (15 MEMBERS)

municipalities (towns). The remaining 51 percent, known as *Federacija Bosna i Herzegovina* (Federation of Bosnia and Herzegovina, or FBiH), is predominately populated by Croats and Muslims and has ten municipalities (called Cantons). The country itself is generally referred to simply as Bosnia (or BiH), and consists of both of these entities.

Representing the People

The local and the central governments are organized along ethnic lines, with the idea that each ethnic group feels more fairly represented if it has equal representation in all public offices.

The birth of any new country is difficult, and BiH is no exception. Critics of the Dayton Agreement have pointed out that ethnic divisions can make problems worse because they continue to focus on differences among peoples. Despite the criticism, however, the government has been relatively successful.

Sarajevo: Did You Know This?

Sarajevo is home to both the central (BiH) and regional federation governments (FBiH). When Bosnia declared independence from Yugoslavia, Serb forces bombed the city. During the three-year siege, thousands of people were killed and many more were forced to flee. Today the city is emerging from the rubble. Many buildings and roads have been rebuilt, and others are in progress.

Historically, Sarajevo is known for its spirit of tolerance. Muslims, Croats, Serbs, Gypsies, Jews, and other ethnic and religious groups all lived together in peace. Though this peace was shattered by the recent civil war, the capital's citizens are proud of their heritage of tolerance and seek to rebuild their multi-ethnic community.

General Population: 415,693*

Ethnic Population: predominately Bosniak (Muslim) and Croat

Year Founded: 1477

Altitude: 1,800 feet (549 m)

Average Daily Temperatures: January 30°F (−1°C); July 68°F (20°C)

*Note: Due to population shifts during the war, all figures are approximate.

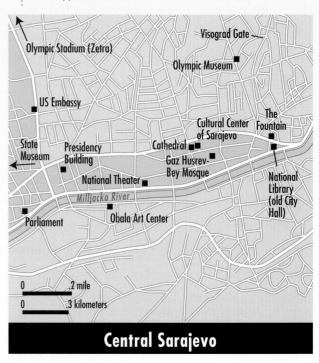

Central Sarajevo

The central government of BiH is like an umbrella covering two semi-autonomous entities. The responsibilities of the central government include foreign policy, international trade, and rebuilding the country. The capital is Sarajevo.

The central government of BiH has three presidents, one for each of the three main ethnic groups: Muslim (also called Bosniak), Croat, and Serb. The presidents are elected by popular vote and serve four-year terms. Every eight months, each president takes a turn as a chairman.

Underneath the tripartite (three-part) presidency are the prime minister and the council of ministers. The presidents appoint a prime minister who must be approved by the House of Representatives. The prime minister appoints a council of ministers. These ministers are responsible for specific matters such as healthcare, finance, and transportation. Just as the U.S. presidency is checked and balanced by a Senate and House of Representatives, so too is the presidency of BiH.

The government has two houses: the House of Representatives, with forty-two members, and the House of Peoples, with fifteen members. Members of both houses are elected by popular vote and serve two-year terms. The House of Representatives has twenty-eight members from the Federation of BiH and fourteen from the Republic of Srpska. The smaller House of Peoples has five Bosniaks, five Serbs, and five Croats.

The two semi-independent entities (Federation of Bosnia and Herzegovina and Republic of Srpska) have their own local governments, each with a slightly different structure. FBiH represents two groups, Croats and Bosniaks. They have two

French marines line up in a trench as members of UNPROFOR.

U.S. and Russian soldiers, members of SFOR, in Bosnia during a live fire artillary exercise.

presidents, one for each ethnic group. Presidents are elected by popular vote and serve a term of two years. Under the presidency are two houses: House of Representatives and the House of the People. As for RS, they have one president elected for a two-year term, and a national assembly with eighty-three elected members each serving for two years.

International Presence

In the early years of the war, the United Nations sent a peacekeeping force called UNPROFOR (United Nations Protection Forces) to the region. Referred to as the "blue helmets" because of the color of their headgear, the forces could not simply pull out of Bosnia after a peace deal was signed. Why? It would take time for the country's anger, distrust, and fear to fade. Bosnia needed a buffer, some force to absorb the shock of change and to help keep the peace.

Many international groups helped cushion the blow of reorganizing and helped foster change in Bosnia. Among them is SFOR (stability force), the military force that replaced UNPROFOR. SFOR is a combined military force made of troops from thirty-four different countries. In 1995, it had about 60,000 troops in Bosnia. By 2002 the number was 12,000—proving that peace in BiH is indeed possible.

Bosnia is rebuilding with some help from the international community. So long as the governmental leaders choose negotiation over war, Bosnia is well on the road to being a multinational, peaceful place to live.

Three Flags Fly

Just as the states within the United States fly their own flags in addition to the national flag, so too do the semi-autonomous entities in Bosnia.

The Republic of Srpska's flag (above) is the same as Serbia's flag: three horizontal stripes of red, blue, and white. RS also displays a coat of arms that hails from the Nemanja Dynasty of the twelfth century. A double-headed white eagle, a mythical creature, stands against a red background and wears a crown. On its shield are four Cs—which stand for Samo Sloga Srbina Spasava. This means united Serbs stand. (If you're wondering why the letter C appears but the slogan of each word begins with an S, it's because Serbians use two alphabets. One is Roman, the kind you're reading here, and the other is Cyrillic, which uses some different letters. (The C in Cyrillic is actually pronounced like an S.)

The flag of the Federation of Bosnia and Herzegovina combines designs from the two ethnic groups it represents: Croat and Muslim. It has three vertical stripes of red, white, and green. In the middle of the flag is a coat of arms with three elements. The top left of the flag has a golden lily on a green background, symbols used by the Kotromanic family, which ruled Bosnia in the fourteenth century. The top right has the historical Croat coat of arms, with twenty-five red and white square fields. The blue bottom has ten white stars forming a circle.

The national flag of Bosnia and Herzegovina has a blue background with a yellow triangle and a line of white stars (below). The triangle represents the three main ethnic groups: Muslim, Serb, and Croat. The color yellow is considered neutral because none of the ethnic groups historically used yellow as a dominant color in their national symbols. The stars at the top and bottom of the flag are cut in half. If the flag were folded so that the two stars touched each other, they would become one complete star. This stands for the desire for both halves of Bosnia, the Serbian Republic and the Federation of BiH, to someday join as one unified whole.

Economy
Past, Present,
and Future

A typical medieval view of peasants farming in the shadow of the feudal castle.

Centuries ago, Bosnia's economy was based on agriculture and mineral mining. Large-scale farming was structured under the feudal system. In this system, peasants could not own any land, but they were allowed to live on and farm the land. In exchange, they had to pay taxes to landowners. They paid with what they produced, giving large percentages of their crops and livestock to the owners. The feudal system was once common throughout Europe and was one of the main ways in which kingdoms and empires enriched themselves.

Today, farming and mineral mining are still important to Bosnia's economy. Bosnia has large deposits of bauxite (used to make aluminum), as well as iron ore, coal, copper, and zinc.

Modern farming equipment is used on large farms in Bosnia.

Opposite: In Bosnia, agricultural projects are supported by foundations to help rebuild the country.

Bosnia has also been known for its logging and furniture production, and it produced much of the former Yugoslavia's weapons. The 1992–1995 war, however, destroyed many factories and farms and completely ruined the economy.

Since 1995 many factories, towns, and cities have been rebuilt. However, much work remains. Reconstruction projects have created some jobs, but unemployment remains high—in some areas as high as 40 percent. International aid and loans help Bosnia rebuild everything from small businesses to banks. Bosnia's well-educated population makes it especially attractive to foreign investors and companies.

Transition to Privitization

In the post-communist era of the 1980s and 1990s, central and eastern European countries, including Bosnia, were in economic transition. Among the economic changes was the move toward greater privatization. The Bosnian government today is pushing for more and larger companies to be privatized. The process allows people and corporations to own businesses that were formerly owned by the government. The government in turn makes money by selling businesses it owns. Under communism, nearly all businesses and industries are government-owned. Tito's looser style of communism allowed for some small privately owned businesses in Yugoslavia and Bosnia. Cafés (*kafanas*),

In Bosnia, cafés were one of the first types of businesses owned privately by individuals and not the government.

popular gathering places for people throughout BiH, were among the first privately owned businesses. Large scale privatization is a new business model for Bosnia, and it is having a positive effect on the economy.

Agriculture

Agriculture is an important industry in BiH. It is the fertile soil that holds some promise for economic growth as the country struggles to get back on its feet. Cattle, sheep, and chickens are raised as livestock. The meat, milk, and eggs feed the local population and are exported to nearby countries.

Most of the farming in Bosnia is small-scale and in private hands. In the northern regions, farmers grow mainly corn, wheat, oats, and barley. In drier, hotter Herzegovina, the main crops are tobacco, cotton, and fruit.

The agricultural industry supplies about 50 percent of the food Bosnia

Vineyards produce grapes in the warm and dry climate regions of Bosnia.

needs. It must import the rest—especially in post-war Bosnia, after the destruction of land and displacement of people. Land mines, still scattered throughout the country, prevent farming in certain areas. Villages that were once rich with crops are slowly returning to their pre-war yields. Many farmers fled during the war and have yet to return to their homes. Some may never come back.

Landmine Removal Expense

Estimates reveal that up to 4 million landmines and booby traps were left behind during the 1992–1995 war. During the twelve-month period of July 1998–June 1999, the United Nations required nearly $40 million for demining activities. Many international donors helped including the World Bank, the U.S. government, the European Union, the Norwegian People's Aid, SFOR, and a collection of smaller, non-governmental organizations. Activities funded by the donors included mine awareness training, mine information and minefield marking, clearance, training, administrative staffing, and operational costs.

If no landmines and booby traps remained in Bosnia, it is estimated that agricultural production would increase by at least 11 percent.

Bosnia was among the poorest republics in Yugoslavia. As part of Yugoslavia, its economy was based on the socialist policies of communist dictator Josip Broz Tito. Still, compared to other communist countries, Bosnia had advantages in its link with Yugoslavia.

Tito broke away from the strict communist economic policies of the Soviet Union and made Yugoslavia the most prosperous of the socialist countries. Health care, higher education, and industrialization were key to his economic plans. From 1957 to 1960, Yugoslavia's economy was the second fastest-growing in the world.

Tito's reforms produced nothing short of an economic revolution. BiH's economy shifted from agriculture to a more modernized industrial economy. For example, in 1947, agriculture accounted for 36 percent of the republic's economy. Industry ranked far behind agriculture. Thirty years later, the numbers were reversed. Agriculture accounted for less than 10 percent of the economy, while industry climbed to 40 percent.

Industrialization brought mechanized factories to Bosnia. The machines in the factories helped produce goods more quickly but still required many workers. Factories boosted the economy and employed

Factories in Bosnia, such as this bottling plant, raise production rates and employ many.

Measuring Value

Many countries measure the growth of their economies using a measurement called Gross Domestic Product (GDP). How does a country figure out its GDP? They calculate the value of the dollar (or other currency unit) for the products they make and the services they perform. The result is a number that lets them see how they are doing from year to year.

In 1997, the growth rate for BiH was a very healthy 37 percent. That was because BiH received a lot of post-war rebuilding money from other countries. Their growth rate has since slowed down; in 2000 it was 10 percent.

We can get a better understanding of what war did to the economy of BiH by comparing its GDP figures before and after the war. In 1990, the GDP was $10.7 billion; post-war, in 1997, it was $3.4 billion. It is certainly good news that the economy is growing, but it's clear that the country has a long way to go before it recovers from the effects of war.

many people. Today's plants produce steel products, processed food, and manufactured pharmaceuticals.

Though factories were state-owned under Tito, workers did have some influence in how things were run. Tito created elected workers' councils, which shifted some control from central government to the councils. The government, however, still set wages. Unfortunately, many of the factories and companies were overstaffed and poorly managed, so product quality declined.

During the 1980s, the economy took a turn for the worse. When Tito died in 1980, politicians scrambled for power. His death wasn't the only reason why the economy began to crumble, however. The country also suffered from food shortages, inflation, job cuts, and financial scandals. As politicians argued about how the country should be governed, the government itself became more unstable. Yugoslavia began to fall apart. Several republics, including Bosnia, sought independence, and as we have seen, Bosnia's declaration had

disastrous results. To gain a better understanding of BiH's economic capabilities, we need to explore the pre-war industries, because many of them are now making a comeback.

A leading industry in Bosnia is chemical production. This is a chemical plant in Tuzla, Bosnia.

How Bosnia Makes Money

About half of BiH's pre-war economy was based on agriculture and heavy industry. The remaining economic activities were in the service sector, such as transportation, education, and media. All this came to a virtual standstill during the war, but many are now recovering quite nicely.

Chemicals and pharmaceuticals were among the leading industries, producing such products as sodium carbonate, liquid chlorine, and soap/detergents. Bosnia's natural resources

Resources

Croplands		B	Bauxite
Mixed farming		C	Coal
Pastures		Cu	Copper
Forest		I	Iron
		L	Lignite
		S	Salt

include minerals and trees, so it exported large amounts of lumber to other republics, including Croatia and Slovenia, for further processing. Furniture was and still is a vital industry in BiH.

Bauxite, a mineral found in soil, is plentiful in BiH. Bauxite is used to make aluminum. Plants in Mostar and Zvornik are near major bauxite deposits. Many products such as metal wires, bars, and ingots were exported to Croatia, Slovenia, and Russia. Automakers Fiat and Daimler Benz were major customers.

The country is also rich in non-metal minerals, including rock salt, high-quality clays, and dolomite, which is used in the production of steel. The economic potential of these resources is promising.

Foreign companies assist the Bosnian economy by establishing factories and hiring local workers. For example, the

Lumber Industry

Nearly half of Bosnia is covered in forest. The lumber industry is big business in Bosnia; it's among the top money makers in the country. More than 1,500 companies, large and small, cut lumber. Sawmills produce about 600,000 cubic meters of lumber each year.

Most of the lumber comes from hardwood trees such as beech and oak. Soft wood, such as pine and spruce, is also cut and sold. To prevent over-harvesting, the industry is carefully managed and trees are regularly replaced.

Coca-Cola® company established a relationship with a local brewery in Sarajevo. Competitor PepsiCo®, licensed a beverage company in Banja Luka to manufacture its product. Competition, a basic ingredient of a market-driven economy, is clearly becoming a part of business life in BiH.

Though there aren't many advertising agencies in BiH, it is considered an area of growth. Currently, radio, television, and (to a lesser extent) newspapers and magazines are the primary ways that businesses advertise goods and services. Large billboards, once uncommon in BiH, are beginning to appear on main thoroughfares.

A billboard in Sarajevo advertises a company's product in a big way.

What Bosnia Grows, Makes, and Mines

Agriculture

Corn	900,000 metric tons
Wheat	275,000 metric tons
Fruit	128,000 metric tons

Manufacturing (2003 est.)

Automobiles	38,000 units
Tractors	34,000 units
Television receivers	21,000 units

Mining (1997 est.)

Lignite	1,640,000 metric tons

An office building under repair

From Reconstruction to Reform

The war may have ended after three years, but the damage it created continues well beyond the 1995 Dayton Peace Agreement. In the years immediately following the war, the country concentrated on rebuilding homes, factories, and basic infrastructures such as power plants, roads, and bridges.

The two entities, Republic of Srpska and the Federation of Bosnia and

Units and Measures

BiH uses the metric system. The basic values are:

1 pound = 0.45 kilograms

1 mile = 1.6 kilometers

1 gallon = 3.78 liters

80°F = 26°C

If you weigh 125 pounds, your weight in kilograms is 56.25. The equation looks like this: 125 pounds x .45 kilos. How many kilos do you weigh?

Herzegovina, have a long way to go to create unified economic standards. For example, they have different privatization laws and different currencies—not unusual in a new country. All countries develop, change, and adapt over time, and the most disorganized years are the early ones. In the short time that Bosnia has existed as a new country, it has experienced economic growth. That's a positive sign for the future.

Money Facts

BiH has two kinds of banknotes, one for the Federation of BiH and another for the Republic of Srpska. Both can be used in either republic and both are "convertible Marks" (Konvertibilna Marka or KM) based on the German deutsche mark. One KM is equal to one deutsche mark. One U.S. dollar equals 2.04KM. The denominations and even the color of the bills are the same in RS and FbiH currency, but the images differ.

Only one version of coins is used by both RS and FbiH. It includes 1KM and 2KM and fenings. One hundred fenings equal 1KM. The nickel-plated steel 1-KM coin carries the national BiH coat of arms on the center back and has a bold 1KM imprinted on the front. One indented and inverted triangle appears on the top and bottom of both sides of the coin, so that sight-impaired people can easily tell its value. The 2-KM nickel-brass coin has a dove of peace on the back and "2KM" on the front. It has two indented and inverted triangles.

Note: The German deutsche mark has been phased out in Germany and replaced by the Euro.

One Country, Three Ethnic Groups

72

THE FIRST KNOWN INHABITANTS OF BOSNIA WERE CALLED the Illyrians who lived in the era before the birth of Christ. This group was eventually absorbed into the Roman Empire.

Opposite: **Bosnia's population consists of various Slavic groups that settled in the area over the centuries.**

Today, the people of Bosnia are mostly Slavs. Slavs include many different groups; for example, Slovenians, Serbians, Croatians, and Bulgarians are Slavs. All share a common ancestry. The major ethnic groups currently in Bosnia are Bosniaks (Bosnian Muslims), Serbs, and Croats. The Muslims make up almost half the population. Though all are Slavs, different types of Slavs identify very closely with their particular ethnic group. Most Bosnians refer to themselves according to their ethnic group. For example, they say they are Bosnian Croat, Bosnian Serb, or Bosnian Muslim or Bosniak.

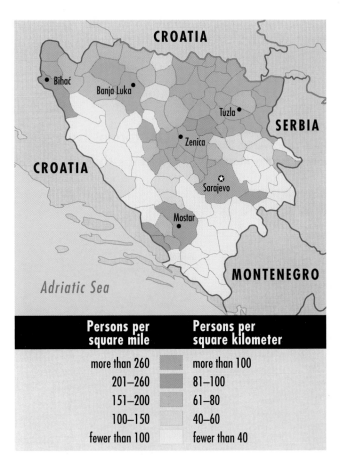

The Slavs in Bosnia

The original Slav settlers migrated to Bosnia from northeastern Europe. The settlers formed villages and communities that were changed over time by the empires that conquered

Population of Major Cities	
Sarajevo	387,876
Banja Luka	218,436
Mostar	208,904
Tuzla	118,500

them. The most influential were the Roman/Byzantine, Ottoman Turks, and Hapsburg/Austro-Hungarian Empires. These empires influenced Bosnian social customs, religious beliefs, art, and culture. The empires also affected the profile of the population.

With each empire, the ethnic makeup of the population changed. Some of those who lived in Bosnia ran away from the invading empires and some were killed, but many stayed. Each empire introduced unique customs and new ethnic groups, including Turks, Austrians, and Hungarians. You can find their influence in the art, architecture, food, and language of Bosnia.

Slavs and Their Ethnic Groups

Muslims in Bosnia, descendants of converted Slavs, pray at the Bey Mosque.

Historians believe that the Slavs are descendants of migrant groups that traveled through the Carpathian Mountains and settled in various regions of the Balkans, including Bosnia and Herzegovina. The Slavs that settled in the north and along the coast called themselves Croats. Those that moved to the middle and southern areas called themselves Serbs. The Muslims that live in Bosnia today are considered by most to be the descendants of Slavs (mostly Serbs or Croats) who converted to Islam during the Ottoman Empire.

These groups share some social customs, but they also have their own unique practices. Many customs developed from the different religions of the three groups. In general, Muslims (or Bosniaks) are Mulsim, Serbs are Christian Orthodox, and Croats are Roman Catholic.

Understanding Ethnic Ties

As we have seen, Bosnia and Herzegovina was once a republic within Yugoslavia. For many years, Yugoslavia was a communist country whose leader encouraged citizens to call themselves Yugoslavs instead of identifying with a particular ethnic group. It was an attempt to reduce the troublesome ethnic tensions, especially between Serbs and Croats.

Wars Cause Migrations

Refugees from war are as common today as they were centuries ago. The 1992–1995 war in Bosnia caused a massive population shift. Communities that were once of mixed ethnic origin now consist mostly of a single ethnic group.

Bosnian Croats celebrate their national pride by waving their flag.

Of Bosniaks and Bosnians

Recently, the Muslims of BiH have been called Bosniaks. Why not simply call themselves Muslims? The political leaders of the Muslims sought a non-religious name for their group, just as Serbs and Croats have.

Some resisted using the term Yugoslav; others embraced it. To call yourself a Yugoslav is similar to calling yourself an American or a Canadian: neither title has an ethnic tie. Why all the fuss over a label? It has to do with individual and group identity. The people of Yugoslavia came from territories where their ethnic groups formed the majority of the population. For example, the majority of people who live in Serbia are Serbs, and the majority of people who live Croatia are Croat. Naturally, when Serbia and Croatia became a part of Yugoslavia, people still saw themselves as Serbs and Croats.

The desire to identify with a particular ancestry is common throughout the world, even in so-called melting pot countries such as the United States. Think of how often you hear someone described with a hyphenated identity—for example, Mexican-American, Irish-American, or African-American. It's interesting and fun to take pride in the culture and ethnic group of your ancestors. The problem occurs when politicians manipulate people and spread lies about other groups for their own personal gain. Such has been the case in the Balkans (and elsewhere) for ages.

The creation of Yugoslav was an attempt to unite people of different republics and ethnic groups. By calling all citizens Yugoslavs, the government sought to set aside ethnic differences. It was a great idea when Yugoslavia was Yugoslavia. It even worked to some degree. The more educated people were more likely to call themselves Yugoslavs. But when Tito died in 1980, he left no clear direction for how the country would proceed. There was a rotating presidency representing the different ethnic groups, but some politicians sought to grab complete power.

Many politicians were quick to appeal to ethnic identities again. They stirred up trouble by spreading lies about other ethnic groups and creating fear among friends and neighbors of different ethnicities. By doing so, they hoped to rally a particular ethnic group and get more of its votes. Appealing to ethnic origins was an easy way for politicians to gain control and power.

Where clear ethnic majorities existed in the former Yugoslav republics, the problems were fewer. In Bosnia, however, there was and still is no overwhelming ethnic majority.

Creating ethnic identities within Bosnia's population has created a divided people.

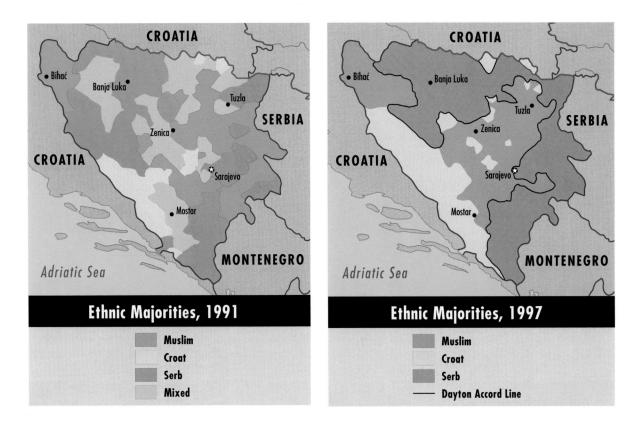

Ethnic Majorities, 1991

- Muslim
- Croat
- Serb
- Mixed

CROATIA
Bihać
Banja Luka
Tuzla
SERBIA
Zenica
CROATIA
Sarajevo
Mostar
MONTENEGRO
Adriatic Sea

Ethnic Majorities, 1997

- Muslim
- Croat
- Serb
- — Dayton Accord Line

CROATIA
Bihać
Banja Luka
Tuzla
SERBIA
Zenica
CROATIA
Sarajevo
Mostar
MONTENEGRO
Adriatic Sea

Politicians scrambled for power and divided the people. Communities that were once of mixed ethnicity have been reorganized along ethnic lines, as the maps clearly show.

The People Paid Dearly

The 1992–1995 war cost the people of Bosnia dearly: approximately 250,000 people were killed, more than 200,000 were wounded, 13,000 were permanently disabled, and thousands became refugees. Many of the displaced have yet to return to their homes. Most never will.

Politics of Language

Politics are a part of life in Bosnia. To avoid offending any one group, the government lists three official languages for Bosnia and Herzegovina: Bosnian, Serbian, and Croatian. They are all basically the same language. Linguists (people who study languages) call the language Serbo-Croatian. The differences among Bosnian, Serbian, and Croatian languages are like the differences between the English spoken in America and the English spoken in Great Britain. It is really a difference in dialect, where some words are spelled and pronounced a bit differently. For example, coffee is *kava* in Croatian but *kafa* in Serbian and Bosnian. Serbians use two alphabets, one with Roman letters (which is what you are reading now) and another with a Cyrillic alphabet.

German and English are also widely spoken, especially in the cities. English words have made their way into the Serbo-Croatian language as well. For example, computer in Serbo-Croatian is *komputer*.

Common Phrases

Dobro Došli (doh-bro dosh-lee)	Welcome
Dobro jutro (doh-bro you-tro)	Good morning
Dobar dan (doh-bar dahn)	Good day
Zdravo (zdrah-voh)	Hello
Kako si? (kah-ko see)	How are you?
Sta ima? (shsta emah)	What's up?
Do videjenja (Doh vee-jehna)	Goodbye
Ciao (chow)	Bye

Saints Cyril and Methodius created a language that became the base of the Cyrillic alphabet that is used in Bosnia today.

Brothers Build a Common Language

Brothers Cyril and Methodius were Greek Byzantine missionaries. Centuries ago they and other Greek missionaries spread Orthodox Christianity to their Slav neighbors. The Slavs all spoke a similar language, but used different dialects. So that the Slavs could better understand the Orthodox teachings, the brothers developed a church language called Old Slavonic. Old Slavonic became the foundation for the Cyrillic alphabet.

Try Cyrillic

Using the letters in the box below, try writing your name using Cyrillic letters. For example, Lana, a common Serbian name for a girl, would be written as Лана. What would your name look like?

An Alphabet Comparison

The Roman Alphabet	The Cyrillic Alphabet	Pronounced As In
A a	A a	f<u>a</u>ther
B b	Б б	<u>b</u>eg
C c	Ц ц	lo<u>ts</u>
Č č	Ч ч	<u>ch</u>ime
Ć ć	Ћ ћ	<u>t</u>une
D d	Д д	<u>d</u>og
Dž dž	Џ џ	<u>j</u>oy
Đ đ	Ђ ђ	<u>de</u>w
E e	E e	m<u>e</u>n
F f	Ф ф	<u>f</u>ish
G g	Г г	<u>g</u>ood
H h	X x	<u>h</u>is
I i	И и	sh<u>e</u>
J j	J j	<u>y</u>ou
K k	K k	<u>k</u>ind
L l	Л л	<u>l</u>ake
Lj lj	Љ љ	mil<u>li</u>on
M m	M m	<u>m</u>oon
N n	H н	<u>n</u>ot
Nj nj	Њ њ	on<u>io</u>n
O o	O o	d<u>oo</u>r
P p	П п	<u>p</u>en
R r	Р р	<u>r</u>un
S s	C c	<u>s</u>on
Š š	Ш ш	<u>sh</u>e
T t	T т	<u>t</u>ag
U u	У у	r<u>u</u>le
V v	В в	<u>v</u>ery
Z z	З з	<u>z</u>oo
Ž ž	Ж ж	lei<u>su</u>re

One Country, Three Ethnic Groups **81**

Families are important to the people of BiH, no matter what their ethnic orientation may be. Young people tend to live with their parents much longer than those in the United States. If children go to a university in their own city, they will often live at home rather than in their own apartments.

Family ties are strong in Bosnia.

Kisses Two and Three

When Bosniaks or Croats greet each other, they kiss one another's cheeks, giving one kiss on each cheek. Serbs kiss each other's cheeks three times—left, right, then left again. This type of greeting is most common among good friends and family members. But you might even see business or political people greet each other this way.

They do this to save money and because there is a shortage of available housing. Also they feel no cultural pressure to leave home early. Most young people in BiH live at home until they marry.

It is also common for extended families to live near one another or even in the same home. Having aunts, uncles, and cousins nearby provides people with plenty of family attention and affection.

Common Names in Bosnia

Muslim girls: Azra, Ira
Serbian girls: Nina, Radmila
Croatian girls: Silvija, Natalia

Muslim boys: Aziz, Damir
Serbian boys: Dragan, Milan
Croatian boys: Franjo, Danko

Three Faiths

84

MOST PEOPLE AROUND THE WORLD BELIEVE IN A HIGHER power and practice some form of religion. Religions define moral behaviors and how people observe life experiences such as births, deaths, and marriages. Each religion has specific codes of conduct and unique ways of acknowledging important events and holidays. About 2 billion people in the world practice Christianity, 1.2 billion follow Islamic teachings, and nearly 15 million devote themselves to Judaism. All three of these religions exist in Bosnia, which has long prided itself on religious tolerance.

The most practiced religions in Bosnia are: Islam, Orthodox Christianity, and Catholicism. The latter two are

Opposite: **Medieval stone church tower in Mostar**

Religious Communities

Muslim	43%
Orthodox Chrisian	30%
Catholic	18%
Other	9%

Christians pray at a statue of the Virgin Mary.

Christian-based religions. Followers believe that Jesus Christ was the son of God. The followers of Islam are called Muslims. They recognize Jesus as a prophet or messenger of God, but they do not consider him the son of God.

Most of the people who live in Bosnia are of Slavic descent. Through time, the Slavs split into various ethnic groups. Serbians generally follow Orthodox Christianity, while Croatians are traditionally Catholic. How they ended up following these particular branches of Christianity has to do with geography and with the influence of the empires that controlled the land where they lived.

Historically, Croatians lived in the northern and coastal part of the Balkans, where the Roman Empire and the Roman Catholic Church were more influential. The Serbians lived in the central and southern regions, where the Byzantine Empire and Orthodox Christianity were more dominant.

Muslim men read the Koran at the Gazi Husrev-Bey Mosque.

According to most historians, the Bosnian Muslims are also Slavs who converted to Islam during the reign of the Ottoman Empire. During Ottoman rule, Muslims were privileged members of society. To be Muslim at that time had distinct advantages that had nothing to do with religious practice.

The Ottomans believed that religion defined a person's true identity, so they organized their society according to religious affiliation. For example, Muslims from various lands such as Bosnia, Turkey, and Algeria were all part of the same "millet" (which means nation). The fact that they lived in different countries and spoke different languages didn't matter. They were all part of the same Muslim millet. Each religion had its own millet. There was a Muslim millet, a Christian millet, and a Jewish millet. The Ottomans required that each group obey certain rules of conduct and dress.

Not surprisingly, the Muslim millet was at the top of the social ladder. They held the most power and were the only ones permitted to own land and weapons. Christians and Jews

Sharing Prophets

The prophet Abraham is important to Christians, Muslims, and Jews. Scholars credit Abraham as the first to preach about one god at a time when polytheism (belief in many gods) was common. Christianity, Islam, and Judaism share the belief in one god and recognize Abraham as a messenger of that god. Other prophets of Christianity and Judaism are also prophets of Islam, such as Noah, Moses, and Isaac.

Religious Tolerance

Thousands of people sought refuge in Ottoman lands, including Bosnia, when their own countries mistreated them because of their religious beliefs. The Ottomans allowed such refugees to enter, no matter what their faiths were. Though the 1992–1995 war caused great friction among religious groups, religion really didn't have much bearing on the conflict. Bosnia has been known as a place where people of different religions can live peacefully. Today, it seeks to rebuild its reputation as a country that accepts everyone and every religion.

A sixteenth century illustration of janissaries, or Ottoman soldiers who were a high-ranking fighting unit.

were on lower social rungs, had fewer rights, and had to show signs of respect to Muslims. Even though Muslims were of a higher social status, members of other millets were free to worship as they pleased and were not persecuted or harassed for it.

Though birth placed you into a particular millet in the Ottomon Empire, you could convert. Many people renounced their Christian faith to become Muslims, because the conversion improved their social standing. Many followers of the Bogomil religion also converted to Islam.

Not all conversions were voluntary. During the fifteenth and sixteenth centuries a system of forced conversions was in place. Ottomans kidnapped children, converted them to Islam, and educated and trained them to be *janissaries*, or Ottoman soldiers. The janissaries made up an elite fighting force and made the Ottoman Empire even more powerful.

Bogomilism

The Bogomil religion was popular in Bosnia until the fifteenth century. Historians think that many Bogomils converted to Islam when the Ottoman Empire took control of Bosnia.

Bogomilism was a "dualist" religion. Bogomils believed that God created the human soul but that matter, or the physical body, was created by Satan, God's evil son. They believed that the difficulty for people on earth, therefore, was a constant struggle between material-ism (defined also as darkness) and spirit (des-cribed as light). The religion developed in Bulgaria and eventually spread through other parts of the Balkans and Europe.

Stecci (right) is the name of the ancient tombstones that appear in the Bosnian countryside. These 700-year-old memorials are engraved with symbols that depict family life, tribal warriors, the sun, and the moon. The people who made them were followers of Bogomilism.

As we have seen, the empires that ruled over Bosnia brought their own religions that greatly influenced the people that they governed. Though it was not an empire, communism affected religious practice in Bosnia too. It drove many people away from regular religious practice. Tito downplayed the importance of religion. Many people avoided going to formal religious services during his dictatorship. Religious beliefs did not die, however; many people continued to celebrate special holidays privately with families and friends.

Religions provide followers with more than a spiritual practice. They also bond people together in a community. After the 1992–1995 war, people found renewed interest in their religions, and attendance in churches and mosques increased.

Following a religion is a matter of degree. Some people choose to strictly obey religious law, while others are more liberal in their devotion. This is as true for Muslims as it is for Christians, Jews, and members of other religions. Let's take a look at how the people of Bosnia practice their particular religions.

Muslim Traditions in Bosnia

Bosnian Muslims generally do not follow the strict religious rules commonly practiced by Muslims in the Middle East. For example, Bosnian women are not confined to the home as they are in Middle Eastern countries. They freely go wherever they choose at any time. Bosnian women work outside the home and hold down a variety of jobs, from bus driving to teaching.

Though you will see most residents of villages and smaller towns wearing traditional clothing, most Muslim women in Bosnia wear conventional European clothes instead of traditional loose-fitting garb that covers the body from head to toe. Likewise, men wear fashionable clothes, whereas the Muslim religious code calls for loose, modest clothing that covers the entire body.

Most Muslim women in Bosnia do not wear traditional Islamic dress.

Islam forbids Muslims to drink alcohol or to eat pork products. Yet in Bosnia it is not uncommon for Muslims to consume an alcoholic beverage and enjoy salami, hot dogs, and roast pork.

Whether strictly religious or only mildly so, most Bosnian Muslims celebrate the main holidays, known as the Eids, that occur twice each year: the Eid of Sacrifice (Eid Al-Adhha) and the Eid of Fast Breaking (Eid Al-Fitr), which occurs after the month-long fast of Ramadan. *Eid* means festivity in Arabic. During the Eids Muslims greet each other with an Arabic phrase, *Bajram Mubarek Olsum*, meaning "Happy Eid."

Muslims celebrate Eid-al Fitr, which marks the end of Ramadan.

Mosques

A mosque is a Muslim house of worship. Bosnia has many mosques, some dating from centuries ago. The long slender column that rises on the side of the mosque is called a minaret.

Ramadan falls at different times each year because a lunar calendar is used to determine the date. During the month of Ramadan, Muslims do not eat between sunrise and sunset. After the month is over, they celebrate for three days. Families

Muslim Prayer Call

Five times a day a Mu'azzin calls Muslims to prayer. He climbs to the top of the minaret, and from a window, he loudly chants specific Arabic phrases so that neighbors can hear the call and prepare to pray. His voice can be heard throughout the town or village where the mosque is located.

and friends gather and share specially prepared food and drinks. This feast is a way of thanking Allah (the Muslim word for God) for all he provides. Though no longer religious in nature, Thanksgiving in the United States is similar, in that it is a feast of giving thanks.

The Eid of Sacrifice is celebrated in memory of the prophet Abraham, who was told by God to sacrifice his son, Ishmael. This Eid lasts four days. The main event on the first day signifies the sacrifice aspect of the Eid. Muslims who are able give special meats to Muslims who are less fortunate. Children deliver these packets of meat to various families in their community. In gratitude, the families give the children sweets. On the other three days, families and friends enjoy special meals together.

The Five Pillars of Islam

There are five duties required by all Muslims:

1. To publicly declare that Allah is the one God and Muhammad is his prophet.
2. To pray five times daily: before sunrise, in early afternoon, in late afternoon, immediately after sunset, and before retiring.
3. To give money to the poor.
4. To fast during the month of Ramadan.
5. To make a pilgrimage to Mecca at least once, if not prevented by ill health or poverty.

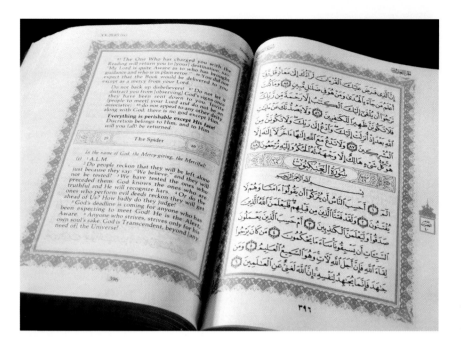

The Koran, Islam's sacred book

Islam's Holy Book

The sacred book of Islam is the Koran (spelled Qur'an in Arabic). It is believed that Allah revealed his teaching to the prophet Mohammed. Initially, the teachings were passed down orally, but the prophet Uthman later wrote them down.

It is also believed that the only way to truly understand the teachings of Islam is to read the Koran in its original language—Arabic. Many people around the world have done so, and it has made the Koran one of the most widely read books in its original language. When a child finishes reading the whole Koran, his or her parents throw a party, called a *bismillah*, to celebrate the accomplishment.

Christians in Bosnia

Almost half the people in Bosnia are Christians, mostly Orthodox (Serbs) or Catholic (Croats). Christianity's main celebrations are

An Orthodox priest celebrates Easter with his parishiners.

Christmas, which honors the birth of Christ, and Easter, which commemorates Christ's resurrection. Christians in Bosnia celebrate these holidays on different dates than Christians in some other countries. The Serbs follow an older calendar, which places Orthodox Christmas on January 7 (December 25 for Catholics and most other Christians); Orthodox Easter generally falls a few weeks after the date of the Catholic holiday.

How the two Christian groups celebrate these two holidays is similar. Christmas Eve is a special time when families go to evening church services. Bountiful feasts of special food are also common to both. The Serbo-Croatian word for Christmas is *Bozic* (BOH-zgheech) it comes from the word for God, *Bog* (Bohg) and translates to "Infant God."

Historically the Franciscan order of monks is very important to the Croatians of Bosnia. The Franciscans are a religious order of the Catholic Church, founded in 1208 by Saint Francis of Assisi in Italy. Franciscans live a simple life and devote their time to preaching and helping others. During Ottoman rule, Franciscan monks helped negotiate better living standards for Christians. Today, they are helping Bosnians to heal from the recent war.

In the Serbian tradition, every family has a patron saint who protects its members. They honor this saint yearly during an event they call a *Slava* (SLA-vah). They prepare special

Major Religious Holidays

Ramadan	month varies
Christmas	December 25
Orthodox Christmas	January 7
Easter	March or April

Mountain Mystery

In 1981, six Croatian children in the town of Medjugorje, Herzegovina, reportedly saw a spirit. But it wasn't just any spirit. They claimed it was the Virgin Mary. Since that time, believers say that the Virgin Mary appears almost daily. The phenomenon has sparked worldwide attention, and Medjugorje has become a major tourist attraction as well as the destination of religious pilgrimages for millions of people. Some people say that the Virgin Mary appears in Medjugorje to help heal wounds from the past.

foods and invite relatives and friends to enjoy the dinner. Before the festivities begin, a priest arrives. He blesses the home, the family, the Slava *kolach* (KOH-lach), which is a special bread, and a bowl of boiled sweetened wheat called *zito* (ZHEE-toe). When a priest cannot come to the home, people have their kolach blessed at their local Serbian church. Slava celebrations occur throughout the year.

Religious Leaders Yesterday and Today

Saint Sava (left) is the patron saint of Serbia. He was born into the royal Serbian Nemanja family in the twelfth century, but gave up his privileged life to pursue spiritual studies. He educated the Serbian people and instilled in them a love for Christianity.

More recently, Friar Ivo Markovic, a Bosnian Franciscan born in 1952 in Susanj, Bosnia, received the Peace Activist Award in 1998 from the Tanenbaum Center for Interreligious Understanding. The award was given for his efforts to foster peace during the civil war of the 1990s.

Artistic
Expressions

THE PEOPLE OF BOSNIA HAVE A LONG ARTISTIC HISTORY. They make music, build elaborate houses of worship, write beautiful poems, paint pictures, and produce fine films. Bosnia has exported its art around the world and has also imported art and culture from other lands. With satellite television in many homes, the people of Bosnia watch news events and entertainment programs produced locally as well as elsewhere in the world. And no teenager in Bosnia is without at least a weekly, if not daily, dose of MTV.

Functional Art

Art can be both beautiful and functional—meaning that there is a purpose for the item outside of beauty for its own sake. Think of things in your home such as china dishes for special occasions, embroidered tablecloths, and carpets with designs on them. These items all have a practical use, but they're also enhanced by designs or artwork. Architecture is another good example of functional art.

Architecture is a major form of artistic expression in Bosnia. The empires that have come and gone have influenced many different kinds of structures. Bosnia contains the architectural remains of the Roman, Byzantine, Ottoman, and Austro-Hungarian empires.

The architecture in Bosnia reveals a glimpse of the influences of past empires.

Expert Weavers

The people of Bosnia have a long-standing reputation as expert carpet weavers. Colors and patterns of carpets can reveal where the weavers live. Each town uses unique shades and shapes. Geometrical shapes, such as squares and zig-zags, are the most common.

Some carpets are so beautiful that they are hung on walls like valued paintings. Some that were made centuries ago are now displayed on museum walls. This woman is designing a carpet for a Sarajevo textile mill.

Bosnia's long history has left it with a number of historic buildings of great beauty and value. The country's architecture reflects its diverse religious cultures: Some Muslim mosques and Catholic and Orthodox churches were built many centuries ago, while others have been rebuilt or were newly constructed after the 1992–1995 war.

For a taste of the old, there's the town of Jajce, where the remains of the only medieval church tower in the Balkans is located. The tower was part of the church of Saint Luke, which was built sometime in the fourteenth century. The tower is a good example of Romanesque architecture, a style that was developed in Italy and is noted for its round arches and very detailed decorations. This style made its way to Bosnia when the Roman Empire occupied the Balkans.

The bell tower in Jajce is representative of Romanesque architecture.

The Ottomans also organized many cities and influenced the styles of buildings inside and out. They did not allow Christians to build new churches, but they let them enhance and maintain already existing ones. Artists decorated inside walls, furniture, and the exterior of churches. The art of making frescoes (paintings on wet plaster) flourished during this time. Interior church walls were covered with images of saints, kings, and religious scenes.

Wood carving was also popular during this era. Many church doors in Bosnia were elaborately carved with religious

Fresco is the art of painting on freshly spread moist plaster. Here is one completed in the thirteenth century.

scenes and symbols. But wood carving was not solely for decoration in churches. Many homes contained carved furniture, staircases, and paneling (wood walls). The city of Mostar contains good examples of traditional homes filled with ornate wood carving, an art that is still practiced today.

The Ottomans organized cities and towns around important public meeting places: mosques, baths, and markets. They introduced covered markets as well. One in Sarajevo was built in 1551. It features thick stone and brick walls and domed ceilings, more examples of art that is both beautiful and functional.

Words

The Ottoman Empire's influence extended beyond architecture. It was also a culture that produced books and introduced bookbinding to Bosnia. Literature was and is very important in this region. Today's writers publish on the Internet as well as in books, magazines, and newspapers.

Nobel Prize-winner Ivo Andric (second from left)

Among the most famous and celebrated writers to come from Bosnia is Nobel Prize winner Ivo Andric. He was born in 1892 in Travnik. He is best known for his novel, *The Bridge on the Drina*. He received world-

Honored Poet

Mak Dizdar of Stolac, Herzegovina is considered among the greatest South Slav poets. He was born in 1917 and died in 1971. His began his writing career as a journalist when he was eighteen. His first collection of poems was published before he turned twenty.

His home in Sarajevo, where he wrote many of his famous poems, has been turned into a museum. His last book, published in 1971, is entitled *Blue River*, after his poem of the same name. Dizdar's image appears on the FBiH 10 KM bank note.

Blue River

No one knows where it is
we know little but it is known

behind the mountain behind the valley
behind the seven behind the eight

and even more wretched and even more weird
over tortuous over bitter

over berry over dogrose
over heat over freeze

beyond foreboding beyond doubt
behind the nine behind the ten

and even deeper and even stronger
beyond silence beyond darkness

where roosters do not sing
where horns are not heard

and even more wretched and even more weird
beyond reason beyond God

there is a blue river
wide it is deep it is

a hundred years wide
a thousand summers deep it is

about its length don't even think
jetsam and flotsam unmending
there is a blue river

there is a blue river—
we had better cross the river.

wide recognition for this work, and in the Republic of Srpska he has been given an even more special honor: his portrait appears on the one KM bank note.

Of the many books about the 1992–1995 war, perhaps the most personally revealing of life in wartime was written by

Eleven-year-old Zlata Filipovic poses with her published diary.

11-year old Zlata Filipovic. The book, *Zlata's Diary*, describes what life was like in Sarajevo during the war: having to stay indoors, hiding from windows for fear of snipers, and appreciating essentials like electricity and running water that we usually take for granted.

War Theater

The work of famed poet Mak Dizdar inspired a group of actors to create a theater during the 1992–1995 war. Called SARTR (Sarajevski Ratni Teatar-Sarajevo War Theater), the group first performed during the difficult days of the war, and continues to perform in Sarajevo and abroad.

Aleksandar Hemon is another contemporary writer from Bosnia who now lives in Chicago, Illinois. Hemon traveled to the United States on a journalist exchange program. From there, he watched on television as war broke out in his homeland. He stayed in Chicago working odd jobs, improved his English, and wrote a book called *The Question of Bruno*. Critics have hailed him as one of the finest writers of Eastern Europe. His book is a collection of stories revealing what life was like in Sarajevo, and how it felt to be in America while some of his friends were still in war-torn Sarajevo. The stories are set in Chicago and Sarajevo. His strong images and relaxed style make the stories easy to read.

**Bosnian author
Aleksandar Heman**

Producers and directors bring stories to life on small and large screens and in theaters across Bosnia. Bosnian storytelling on stage and through film has a long history. For such a small place, the country has earned an impressive international reputation for its storytelling talents, especially in film.

Two internationally famous directors come from Bosnia, Emir Kusturica and Danis Tanovic. Kusturica was born in Sarajevo in 1954 and has a long career as writer, director, and producer. His films tend toward the quirky and surreal. A good example of his style is *Arizona Dream*, an American film that features Johnny Depp, Jerry Lewis, and Faye Dunaway.

Bosnian film director Emir Kusturica

Tanovic, born in 1969, studied civil engineering and music but eventually made a living as a documentary director. His film *No Man's Land* is a fascinating portrayal of the Bosnian civil war. In this riveting film, he clearly shows how no one side is completely innocent or completely guilty when it comes to war. This powerful film won many awards, including the Academy Award for Best Foreign Film in 2001. The films of Kusturica and Tanovic are available in video stores in the United States and Canada.

Danis Tanovic holds his Golden Doves for Peace award for his film *No Man's Land*.

National Theater

The National Theater in Sarajevo presents ballet, opera, and dramas throughout the year. The Italian neo-Renaissance building was constructed in 1898 under the Austro-Hungarian Empire. During the 1992–1995 war, brave actors continued to perform, even as bombs exploded around the city.

Music Past and Present

Music is tied to many aspects of daily life. We sing "Happy Birthday" to our loved ones and sing Christmas carols to celebrate the holiday. We also have songs and music for other occasions such as weddings, funerals, and national and religious holidays. Even sporting events are connected to music: Americans sing the national anthem before a ball is thrown, bounced, or kicked.

Folk music is generally considered traditional music, often originating from the countryside. In times past, Bosnia and

Birthday Parties

Children in Bosnia celebrate birthdays with both adults and other children. It's not a kids-only affair, as is often the custom in the United States. Everyone shares in the fun. This is because family members live close to one another and parents are generally friendly with the parents of their children's playmates. As in the United States, no birthday celebration would be complete without gifts and a cake with candles.

Herzegovina had specially developed lyric songs (songs with words) performed in a style called *ganga*. The singers would come from the same village. They performed in small groups of men or women (genders did not mix). The groups would perform together from a very young age into adulthood. This was a time when people generally lived in the village of their birth their whole lives.

Members of a ganga group stood together, shoulder to shoulder, forming a tight semi-circle. Being physically close helped put everyone on the same emotional level. If you've ever sung in a choir, you might know the feeling of singing in a group, and how a kind of energy forms within that group. Ganga singers sang songs of hope, desire, love, and loss.

Gypsies, people who migrated from India a long time ago, form a small part of the Bosnian population, but they are famous for their musical abilities. Traditionally, they traveled from village to village singing songs and playing stringed instruments and tambourines. Most of the Gypsy musicians were male. Villagers sometimes felt uneasy about these wandering male musicians. Their pretty songs and carefree way of life could disrupt conservative life in the village, or worse yet, attract village women.

Cross-Cultural Lute

An instrument called the *saz* has been part of Bosnia's heritage. The saz is a stringed instrument with a very long neck, similar to the lute. It is related to an instrument found in Turkey. It entered Bosnia during the time that the Ottoman Turks ruled the area. The instrument was adopted from the Turkish to the Bosnian culture.

A traditional form of Bosnian folk music that is still popular today is played by *tamburitza* (tOM-buhr-RIT-za) orchestras. The term tamburitza is derived from the Turkish language. The music itself can be traced as far back as the fourteenth century. Tamburitza orchestras play tamburas, which are stringed instruments similar to mandolins. Guitars and stand-up basses are often part of the ensemble. The musicians play in groups of up to ten or more. Their high-energy music and spirited performances make Tamburitza players especially popular for weddings and dances.

Musical Squeeze Box

Traditional Bosnian folk music is also played on the accordion. The accordion made its way to the Balkans from Western Europe. A quartet formed with accordion, guitar, violin, and bass is a common combination.

Popular Bosnian music today is a blend of styles from America, Europe, and traditional Bosnian forms. Radio stations play a broad mix. You might hear an American pop song, a bit of hip hop, or some techno, followed by a traditional Bosnian *sevdalinka*, or love song. Teenagers will listen to music from all over the Balkans, Europe, and especially America. Back Street Boys, Nirvana, Madonna, and Michael Jackson have been tops on many Bosnian teenagers' charts. Professional symphony orchestras are more popular with adults, who go to concert halls to hear classical works.

Traditionally dressed Bosnians dance at the opening of cultural festivities called International Festival Sarajevo.

Move Your Feet

Traditional folk dancing in Bosnia has changed very little over the centuries. The dances are called *kolos* (KOH-lows). Men,

Folk Dancing Beyond Bosnia

Love of Bosnian folk dance has crossed international borders. As immigrants from Bosnia settled in the United States and Canada, they brought traditional dances. Folklore groups are usually organized through churches. Dancers tend to be young, and everyone is welcome—Bosnian-born and otherwise. The traditional costumes are quite beautiful; some are adorned with jangling coins, or include intricately embroidered vests, and pretty veils. Folklore groups often travel to other cities to perform their dances at church-sponsored events.

women, boys, and girls join hands in a semi-circle and dance in a line that snakes around the dance floor. Steps are slow or fast, and are often quite complicated and aerobic. An evening of kolo can be a real workout. People dance kolos today at weddings, festivals, and other special occasions.

Amateur and professional folklore groups in Bosnia are also popular. The groups perform traditional dances that include kolos and other forms. The folklore dance tradition is rooted in Serbian and Croatian culture. Many dances tell stories through movement and in the way that the dancers relate to each other.

For example, in some dances the men and women separate, forming parallel lines facing each other. They dance in a call-and-response manner: the men "call out" with high large steps, the women respond with smaller, more subtle movements. Other dances may highlight performances of male dancers. Each man tries to "out-dance" the others to win a woman's favor. There are also women-only dances, such as the one performed wearing flowing veils, and dances that only men perform, with swords. It's great fun to watch these groups and even more fun to dance in them. Many adults in Bosnia were a part of a folklore group when they were young.

Folk dance certainly isn't the only type of dance in Bosnia. Discos are often packed with people well into early morning. Unlike the United States, where you must be of a certain age to enter a disco or nightclub, Bosnian youths of any age are admitted. It is also socially acceptable for girls to dance with either their girlfriends or with boys, so there's no reason to stand on the sidelines. In discos, people also sing aloud the words of their favorite songs. Professional ballet and modern dance troupes are also part of Bosnia's dance scene.

Enjoying Life

DAILY LIFE IN BOSNIA IS SIMILAR TO LIFE IN THE UNITED States and Canada. People go to work, attend school, raise children, and celebrate holidays with family and friends. Leisure time, however, is greatly valued, so the amount of time off Bosnians have from work is quite generous compared to U.S. standards. Most people get at least three weeks of vacation per year, depending upon their years of service to a company.

Opposite: **A day of leisure in Sarajevo**

Schools are out during the summer months, making it a popular time for families to vacation together. Traveling to the mountains or to the Adriatic coast is common. Many city dwellers also have weekend homes where they can escape the city hustle and bustle and enjoy nature.

In the recent past, life in Bosnia has been quite difficult. The people of BiH are still struggling, ten years after the civil war. For this reason, some people in Bosnia say that they have learned to cherish what it most important to them—time with family and friends.

Play Time

Sports are an important part of leisure life in Bosnia. People travel to Bosnia's many mountains during all seasons. In winter, skiing is a top pursuit, and it has become even more so because of the Winter Olympic Games that took place in Sarajevo in 1984. Before that time, only a select few would brave the hills on skis. Now, however, groomed runs and ski

The High Art of Enjoying Coffee

Ide na Kafu (EYE-deh nah KAH-fu), meaning "let's have coffee," a phrase you'll hear often in Bosnia. Bosnians love their coffee, which is generally served Turkish style. *Turska Kafa* (TOUR-ska KAH-fah), Turkish coffee, is made with finely powered coffee grounds boiled in water. It is served in small espresso cups, complete with the grounds, and the fine powder settles to the bottom of the cup. A cube of sugar often accompanies the coffee. Sometimes people dip the sugar cube in the coffee and eat it, rather than dissolving it the cup. Another common sweet served with coffee is *ratluk* (rot-luke), or Turkish delight, a sweet jellied candy.

Kafanas (kah-FUN-ahs) or cafés (pictured) line the main streets of towns and cities across Bosnia. University students especially enjoy spending time in kafanas. You can often hear students discussing their studies. Many close only after the last customer leaves, which could be very late indeed.

Delighted youngsters sled in Sarajevo.

lifts are common. Children today learn to ski at an early age. Many receive their first skis, poles, and bindings as gifts during the winter holiday season. Avid skiers purchase seasonal lift tickets and enjoy the slopes all winter long. Ice skating and sledding are also popular winter pursuits.

In summer, hikers wander the many trails that snake through Bosnian hills. Hunters and fishermen also flock to the countryside to catch fish and track down bears, birds, deer, and other game.

Skiing Olympic Slopes

Sarajevo was the host city to the Fourteenth Winter Olympics. The mountains are perfect for winter sports, especially skiing. They are snowy most of the winter, with beautiful evergreen trees lining the runs. Skiiers from BiH and around Europe visit the city and enjoy the slopes. The prices are more reasonable than elsewhere in Europe and the runs are superb. The Jahorina and Bjelasnica Olympic Ski centers operate each winter from December through March. They are among the most popular ski slopes.

Sarajevo is not content to just remember the 1984 Olympics—it has its eyes on securing future games. The city plans to bid to become host of the 2010 Winter Olympics.

After school is out for the year, Bosnian boys can be found playing soccer and basketball. Girls tend toward tennis, jump rope, and hopscotch. Many young people also enjoy riding bikes, rollerblading, and skateboarding.

Riding the River

The rivers and lakes around Bosnia provide splashing good times for the young and young at heart. Rafting down the Neretva in Herzegovina is a special treat on hot summer days. The Neretva is called the emerald river because of its color, and eventually spills into the Adriatic Sea. The upper part of the river flows through canyons and wild areas filled with trees and flowers. The lower part of the river has excellent beaches and is a popular holiday spot, where people swim, fish, or simply soak up the sun.

Computers supply the indoor pastime of choice in Bosnia. Surfing the Internet or playing video and computer games keeps many youths occupied for hours. They also play board games familiar to Americans, such as Scrabble® and Monopoly® (in local-language versions).

Korzo

People in Bosnia love to socialize. An evening stroll, called *korzo* (KORH-zoh), is one of the main ways to stay in touch with friends and neighbors. It's also a great way to meet people. In many towns, the main street is closed to traffic in the early evenings so that people can stroll the street, stopping to visit with friends and popping into cafés for refreshments.

Yearly Event Honors Famous Athlete

Among the most popular youth tournaments is the "Days of Drazen Petrovic," held each June in Sarajevo. The event is named for the legendary Croatian professional basketball player who played in Europe and for the Portland Blazers and New Jersey Nets in the U.S. NBA (National Basketball Association). He died in a car accident in 1993 at age 29. His mother Biserka Petrovic hands out the winning trophies.

Cycling Together

Sports teams help unify a community. In Banja Luka, Republic of Srpska, a USAID-sponsored ride included the nearby regions of Zenica, Tuzla, Banja Luka, and Prijedor. The gathering was not a race, but a ride to bring people together. Riders from ages seven to seventy participated in this first post-war multi-community bicycle event. It was cosponsored by the American Refugee Committee, one of many international aid organizations assisting the people of Bosnia through community development.

The more physically active visit local and regional clubs to participate in many sports, including running, cycling, basketball, soccer, and volleyball. Amateur athletes join these clubs for a little exercise, friendly competition, and socializing with people from other towns. Of course, no one minds bringing a trophy home.

Professional sports in Bosnia include basketball and soccer teams. Basketball in particular has been a source of pride for the people of the Balkans. Many players from this part of Europe have achieved international status. Professional games are televised and also aired on local radio stations, and the Federation of Bosnia and Herzegovina and the Republic of Srpska both have professional leagues.

At Work

The workday in Bosnia generally runs from 7 A.M. to 3 P.M. Cars are very expensive in BiH, so most people walk to work or take a bus.

Men and women hold down jobs in every category, from office work to farming to medical and university professions. The people of Bosnia make products for their use and for export into neighboring republics. Two major export products are furniture and medicines.

A journalist hard at work at his desk.

Jobs in BiH aren't as plentiful as they once were, because the economy has been slow to recover from the 1992–1995 war. Many factories and towns were destroyed, and unemployment has been high, up to 40 percent in some areas. Still, people manage. Some have even opened their own businesses. Privately owned businesses are a new and welcome trend in post-communist BiH.

School Days

Compared to U.S. schools, BiH schools are organized differently. Elementary school here is grades one through eight.

Fashion Sense

The people of BiH follow the fashion trends of Europe. Most men and women in Bosnia take great pride in their appearance. For example, women and young girls take their time to style their hair, makeup, and press their clothes before going anywhere—even grocery shopping. Pride of appearance is taught to girls and boys at a young age. Those who want a modeling career can go to modeling school and talent agencies in Sarajevo.

Grade school children only attend class for five hours a day.

The school days for elementary students are shorter than in the United States. Students spend about five hours a day in school. After eight years of elementary school, they attend secondary school. They may choose to attend a vocational school, where they will learn specific trades, such as auto repair or they might attend a college prep school, where they receive education in academic subjects in preparation for university studies.

Mealtime

Prijatno (PREE-yaht-no), which means "enjoy your food," is said before meals. The people of Bosnia certainly do enjoy their meals. Meals are not rushed, but rather savored slowly. The cuisine is a blend of Eastern European, Middle Eastern, and Mediterranean flavors.

Women tend to do most of the food shopping, and they do it almost daily. They go to markets to buy the freshest available fruits, vegetables, and meats. They buy goods in small amounts and replenish their supply when needed. Freshly baked bread is a must and accompanies most meals.

Meal preparation is also the domain of Bosnian women. Fast foods are not the norm; instead women might spend several hours preparing meals from scratch. Tables are often set with ironed white tablecloths and napkins, so that diners feel as

Worth the Wait

Somun (SOH-moon) is a Muslim bread enjoyed especially during the holy days of Ramadan. Children generally have the job of waiting, often in long lines, to purchase the bread. It's a delicious specialty that is well worth the wait.

though they are dining in a five-star restaurant. Microwaves have not yet made it to Bosnia. They may not become very popular, given the preference for preparing meals from fresh foods rather than using canned or frozen choices.

Meals are usually a family affair in Bosnia.

Breakfast usually consists of rolls, butter, jam, perhaps a little ham and eggs, and coffee, tea, or hot chocolate. Children and adults generally eat lunch, their main meal, together at home. The meal is served at about three or four o'clock, much later in the day than most Americans eat lunch. Many different kinds of foods may be eaten for lunch. Favorites include soups, stews, fish, and grilled meats. *Bosanski Lonac* (BO-SAN-ski LOH-nuts), or Bosnian pot, is a slow-cooked stew of meats and vegetables. Dinners are eaten around eight o'clock, and meals are very light. For example, people might eat a little fruit, bread, and cheese, but no main course.

Vegetables alone are not served in large quantities; a salad of tomatoes, onions, and peppers accompanies some meals. Vegetables are, however, used in preparing dishes such as *sarma* (SAR-muh), a spiced meat wrapped in cabbage leaves. A number of traditional dishes feature vegetables stuffed with meat.

Of course, American favorites have made their way to BiH. People enjoy pizza, hamburgers, and of course, Coca-Cola®.

Grilled to Perfection

Meats are a Bosnian staple and a part of most meals. An especially beloved meat dish is *cevapcici* (CHEE-VAHP-chee-chee), a blend of several meats, usually lamb, beef, and pork. The meat is spiced and rolled into small sausages, then grilled over an open flame. You can smell its smokey-sweet scent for blocks. There's no hiding cevapcici. The sausages are served with freshly baked white bread and diced raw onions.

Weddings

In the villages of BiH, weddings have traditionally been elaborate and expensive affairs. Wedding celebrations last several days, and they take place at the bride's home. Guests often stay for days.

After the church ceremony, as Serbian tradition calls for the *kum* (koom), or best man, to throw coins outside the church doors as a symbolic wish for wealth for the couple. Children, of course, love this part of the event, and they scatter to collect the strewn coins. Guests enjoy a great feast of food and drink after the wedding ceremony.

Other commonly eaten foods in Bosnia include a variety of cheeses, served with most meals, and special sweets. A pita is a favorite and is found in bakeries all over BiH. It consists of wrapping meat, cheese, or fruits in thin layers of dough, then baking the pita in the oven until crisp. Baklava is also made with paper-thin layers of dough. In between the layers are a paste of ground nuts, sugar, and honey.

Favorite Beverages

In addition to the beloved coffee, Bosnians enjoy special drinks. A favorite Bosniak drink is *himber* (HIM-behr), a thick juice made from fruits such as raspberries and pears. A special treat is himber made with rose petals, sweetened with sugar, and accented with lemon. Instead of cow's milk, Bosnians often consume a thin yogurt drink.

Other favorites include *slivovitz* (SHLEE-VOH-vitz), a strong plum brandy, and *loza* (LOH-zah), a grape brandy. Many vineyards in Herzegovina make good wines. Bosnian-made brandies and wines are enjoyed by the people of BiH and are also exported to other countries.

You won't go hungry or thirsty when you are in BiH. It is customary to serve guests food and drink when they drop by for a visit. And people feel free to visit one another without calling ahead. It is an open and friendly way of life.

New Year's Celebration

The most festive holiday of the year in BiH is New Year's Eve. Many people buy and decorate evergreen trees complete with lights and ornaments, just like Christmas trees. In Bosnia, people commonly exchange gifts on New Year's Day.

National Holidays

New Year (Gregorian calendar)	January 1
Orthodox Christmas	January 7
Republic Day (Republic of Srpska)	January 9
New Year celebrated by Serbs (Julian calendar)	January 14
Independence Day	March 1
Labor Day	May 1
All Saints Day (Catholic)	November 1
National Day	November 25
Catholic Christmas	December 25

Bosnian Muslims celebrate the following: Month of Ramadan, Ramasa Bairam (feast at the end of Ramadan), Kurban Bairam (feast of sacrifice). Dates vary according to the lunar calendar.

Catholic Easter generally falls in April; Orthodox Easter generally follows a couple of weeks later.

Timeline

Bosnian History

A migrant group settles into the Balkan area known as the south Slavs; this group splits into Croats, Bosnians, and Serbians. — C.E. 6

Hungarian Empire rules. — 1180–1463

Ban Kulin establishes a brief period of independence. — 1180–1204

King Tvrtko rules, proclaims independence, expands Bosnia's territories. — 1353–1391

Ottoman Empire invades and rules Bosnia. — 1463–1875

A peasant rebellion in Herzegovina spreads into neighboring provinces. — 1875

Peasant rebellions lead to the Russo-Turkish war. — 1877–1878

World History

2500 B.C. Egyptians build the Pyramids and the Sphinx in Giza.

563 B.C. The Buddha is born in India.

A.D. 313 The Roman emperor Constantine recognizes Christianity.

610 The Prophet Muhammad begins preaching a new religion called Islam.

1054 The Eastern (Orthodox) and Western (Roman) Churches break apart.

1066 William the Conqueror defeats the English in the Battle of Hastings.

1095 Pope Urban II proclaims the First Crusade.

1215 King John seals the Magna Carta.

1300s The Renaissance begins in Italy.

1347 The Black Death sweeps through Europe.

1453 Ottoman Turks capture Constantinople, conquering the Byzantine Empire.

1492 Columbus arrives in North America.

1500s The Reformation leads to the birth of Protestantism.

1776 The Declaration of Independence is signed.

1789 The French Revolution begins.

1865 The American Civil War ends.

Bosnian History

Austria occupies Bosnia.	1875–1914
World War I dissolves Austro-Hungarian Empire; Kingdom of Serbs, Croats, and Slovenes is formed, with Bosnia as part of this kingdom.	1914–1918
Kingdom renamed Yugoslavia, land of South Slavs.	1929–1991
Croat terrorists assassinate King Aleksandar of Yugoslavia.	1934
World War II and a Yugoslav civil war engulf Bosnia and Herzegovina.	1939–1945
After Soviets kick Tito out of communist community; he develops his own, more liberal version of communism.	1948
Yugoslav president Tito recognizes Bosnia Muslims as having a distinct identity or "nation."	1974
Tito dies; Yugoslav dissolves into chaos as politicians battle for power.	1980
Slobodan Milosevic becomes president of Serbia.	1989
Slovenia declares independence from Yugoslavia; Croatia, and Macedonia follow.	1990
Bosnia declares independence.	1992
Civil war engulfs Bosnia.	1992–1995
Dayton Peace Agreement establishes new borders for Bosnia.	1995
Slobodan Milosevic, former president, and others involved in the civil war are indicted for crimes against humanity.	2000

World History

1914	World War I breaks out.
1917	The Bolshevik Revolution brings communism to Russia.
1929	Worldwide economic depression begins.
1939	World War II begins, following the German invasion of Poland.
1945	World War II ends.
1957	The Vietnam War starts.
1969	Humans land on the moon.
1975	The Vietnam War ends.
1979	Soviet Union invades Afghanistan.
1983	Drought and famine in Africa.
1989	The Berlin Wall is torn down, as communism crumbles in Eastern Europe.
1991	Soviet Union breaks into separate states.
1992	Bill Clinton is elected U.S. president.
2000	George W. Bush is elected U.S. president.
2001	Terrorists attack World Trade Towers, New York and the Pentagon, Washington, D.C.

Fast Facts

Official name: Federation of Bosnia and Herzegovina

Capital: Sarajevo

Sarajevo

Federation of Bosnia and
Herzegovina's flag

Neretva Valley

Official languages:	Bosnian, Serbian, Croatian
Major religions:	Islam, Eastern Orthodox, Roman Catholic
Year of founding:	1995
Government:	Emerging democracy
Chief of state:	Tripartite presidency
Head of government:	Prime minister
Area:	19,741 square miles (51,129 sq km)
Coordinates of geographic center:	44° 00' N, 18° 00' E
Highest elevation:	Mount Maglic, 7,828 feet (2,386 m)
Average temperatures:	70°F (21°C) in July and 32°F (0°C) January
National population:	3,964,388

**Population of
largest cities:**

Sarajevo	415,631
Banja Luka	218,436
Mostar	208,904
Tuzla	118,500

Saint Luke's bell tower

Famous landmarks: ▶ *Cathedral of Jesus' Heart,* Sarajevo

▶ *Jahorina and Bjelasnica Olympic Ski centers,* Sarajevo

▶ *National Theater building,* Sarajevo

▶ *Gazi Husrev-Bey Mosque,* Sarajevo

▶ *Neretva River,* designated by UNESCO as an international natural monument

▶ *Old Mostar bridge,* famous Turkish bridge that arches over the Neretva River, built in 1566, rebuilt after 1992–1995 war

▶ *Romanesque tower of Saint Luke's church,* Jajce

▶ *Stecci,* medieval tombstones scattered around the countryside

▶ *Town of Medjugorje* where the spirit of the Virgin Mary allegedly appears

▶ *Bocka shopping mall,* Banja Luka

Industry: Major primary commodities: wood, coal, minerals
Manufactured products: textiles, clothing and footwear, chemical, electrical and machinery iron, steel and aluminum

Currency: KM (convertible mark)

Weights and measures: Metric system

Literacy rate: 86%

Currency

Bosnian youth

Danis Tanovic

Common Bosnian words and phrases:

Dobro Došli (doh-bro dosh-lee)	Welcome
Dobro jutro (doh-bro you-tro)	Good morning
Dobar dan (doh-bar dahn)	Good day
Zdravo (zdrah-voh)	Hello
Kako si? (kah-ko see)	How are you?
Sta ima? (shsta emah)	What's up?
Do videjenja (Doh vee-jehna)	Goodbye
Ciao (chow)	Bye

Famous people:

Ivo Andric (1892–1975)
Writer

Mak Dizdar (1917–1971)
Poet

Tvrtko Kotromanic (1358–1391)
Bosnia's first king

Emir Kusturica (1954–)
Film director

Fr. Ivo Markovic (1952–)
Bosnian Franciscan peace activist

Gavrilo Princip (1895–1918)
Assassinated Austrian Archduke Ferdinand

Danis Tanovic (1969–)
Film director

To Find Out More

Nonfiction

▶ Black, Eric. *Bosnia, Fractured Region.* Minneapolis, MN: Lerner, 1999.

▶ Filipovic, Zlata. *Zlata's Diary: A Child's Life in Sarajevo.* New York: Viking, 1994.

▶ Yancey, Diane. *Life in War-Torn Bosnia.* Minneapolis, MN: Lucent, 1996.

Web Sites

▶ **Bosnia and Herzegovina**
www.bhtourism.ba
Tourism site for Bosnia, historical, cultural, and sports links.

▶ **World Factbook 2002**
www.cia.gov/cia/publications/
factbook/geos/bk.html
U.S. government statistics and information on Bosnia.

▶ **Bosnian Government Site**
www.fbihvlada.gov.ba
Links to Federation of Bosnia and Herzegovina.

▶ **USAID**
www.usaid.ba/information.htm
*U.S. government mission to
Bosnia site.*

▶ **Goran's Homepage**
walter.cjb.net
*Informal site by a young man
from Bosnia.*

Organizations

▶ **Embassy of Bosnia and
Herzegovina**
2109 E Street NW
Washington, DC 20037

Index

Page numbers in *italics* indicate illustrations.

Meet the Author

JoAnn Milivojevic is a freelance writer and speaker who loves to travel and explore different cultures. Enchantment of the World—*Bosnia and Herzegovina* is her second book for Children's Press. In addition to her exploration of Balkan countries, she also frequently writes about the Caribbean. She initially fell in love with the sea and sand, but it was the people who enticed her to return. Wherever she has traveled, she has found that people are generous and are willing to answer her many questions. A little curiosity goes a long way and has led her to jobs in the Cayman Islands, one of her favorite places to visit. Her travel and cultural stories have appeared in magazines and newspapers nationwide.

JoAnn earned a B.A. in telecommunications from Indiana University and continued her education by pursuing a master's degree in creative writing. In 1980 she began a career in broadcasting. She eventually worked for several television stations as a writer/producer.

Today, she continues to produce select video projects and to write books, magazine articles, and interactive multimedia scripts. Her dog, Tolstoy, is her inspiration and constantly reminds her that roaming the great outdoors is as important to writing as tapping away on the keyboard.

Photo Credits

A Perfect Exposure/Randa Bishop: 7 top, 16, 33, 72, 98

AP/Wide World Photos: 51 top (Joe Marquette), 92, 96, 126 (Sava Radovanovic), 45, 46, 53, 58 bottom, 75, 91, 109, 113, 119, 120, 133 bottom, 133 top

Art Resource, NY: 7 bottom, 36 (Mjeda/ Museum of Historic Treasures of the Ukraine, Kiev, Ukraine), 88 (Snark/ Bibliotheque Nationale, Paris, France)

Bridgeman Art Library International Ltd., London/New York: 103 (Arlije Monastery Church, Serbia, Yugoslavia), 97 (Milseva Monastery, near Prijepolje, Serbia, Yugoslavia)

Corbis Images: 47, 108 (AFP), 80, 38 left (Archivo, Iconografico, S.A.), 43, 48, 61 top (Bettmann), 35 (Bojan Brecelj), 26, 74, 101 (Dean Conger), 58 top (Yves Debay/The Military Picture Library), 2 (Jon Hicks), 37 bottom (Historical Picture Archive), 42, 102, 132 top (Otto Lang), 40 (Michael Maslan/Historic Photographs), 28 (Joe McDonald), 37 top (Gianni Dagli Orti), 51 bottom, 65 (Tim Page), 34 (Chris Rainier), 71, 132 bottom (Reuters NewMedia Inc), 27 (Roger Tidman), 77 (David Turnley), 52 (Peter Turnley), 104 (UPI), 9, 17, 31 top (Michael S. Yamashita)

Corbis Sygma: 107 (Sophie Bassouls), 24 (David Brauchli), 100 (Stephani Cardinale), 116, 125 (Patrick Durand), 112 (Greg English), 83 (Chris Sattleberger), 106 (Les Stone)

Hulton | Archive/Getty Images: 87

Magnum Photos/Thomas Dworzak: 97

Mary Evans Picture Library: 41, 44

National Geographic Image Collection/Dean Conger: 10, 89

Omni-Photo Communications/Peter G. Bussian: 69

Panos Pictures: 20 top (Heldur Netocny), 60 (Clive Shirley)

Peter Arnold Inc.: 19 (Bojan Brecelj/ Still Pictures), 29 top, 30 bottom (Manfred Danegger), 30 top (Lior Rubin), 29 bottom (Gunter Ziesler)

Photo Researchers, NY: 93 (Loirat/ Explorer), cover, 6 (Thouvenin/ Explorer)

Robertstock.com/M Thonig: 56, 130 left

Stock Boston/Peter Menzel: 18

Superstock, Inc.: 20 bottom (Steve Vidler), 8

The Image Works: 95 (James Marshall), 22, 67, 70, 86, 110, 118, 121 (Josef Polleross), 15 (Topham)

TRIP Photo Library: 11, 14, 21, 23, 32, 61 bottom, 62, 63, 64, 85, 131 (M Barlow), 82, 123 (Ibrahim), 84 (M Jenkin), 31 bottom (T Noorits), 78 (H Sayer)

Maps by Joe LeMonnier